Cradle to Grave

Comparative Perspectives on the State of Welfare

RALPH SEGALMAN
Emeritus Professor of Sociology
California State University, Northridge

DAVID MARSLAND
Professor Associate of Sociology
Brunel University

MACMILLAN
PRESS

in association with
THE SOCIAL AFFAIRS UNIT

First published 1989

Published by
THE MACMILLAN PRESS LTD
Houndmills, Basingstoke, Hampshire RG21 2XS
and London
Companies and representatives
throughout the world

Typeset by Wessex Typesetters
(Division of The Eastern Press Ltd)
Frome, Somerset

Printed in Hong Kong

British Library Cataloguing in Publication Data
Segalman, Ralph, *1916–*
Cradle to grave: comparative perspectives
on the state of welfare.—(Studies in
social revaluation).
1. Western world. Public welfare services
I. Title   II. Marsland, David   III. Social
Affairs Unit   IV. Series
361.6′09181′2
ISBN 0–333–47004–4
ISBN 0–333–47005–2 Pbk

Contents

Preface
Digby Anderson

When the Social Affairs Unit was formed in 1980, it chose as its first publication *Breaking the Spell of the Welfare State*. Until then, few social scientists outside economics had been prepared to present the arguments against state welfare and even fewer had had the opportunity to put those arguments to a wide audience. It was not surprising: most sociologists and social policy academics owe their salaries to the welfare state or that branch of it which is state or state subsidised higher education. (Incidentally, it called for and still calls for a degree of courage for a sociologist such as Professor Marsland to criticise state welfare while continuing to teach in the state system.) The fashionable wisdom, reinforced by the enormous vested interest state welfare creates, was that all was well with the welfare state, or would be if yet more taxpayers' money were injected. It is true that Marxists produced 'critiques' of state welfare but only in the name of a utopian state which would run the whole economy on welfare principles.

Today there is general agreement that there is a welfare state problem, even a crisis, though there is much disagreement about its nature and solution. That is some progress. And especially from economists have come studies showing at least the inefficiencies of state welfare, at most its failure to help the poor and the very high cost of that failure. Sociologists, Professors Segalman and Marsland go one further: the welfare state is not just a failure, it causes damage, damage to society and damage to the poor. In combination with 'progressive' policies on divorce and wider 'rights', it subverts the family and local institutions which are potential sources of a welfare far greater than it can deliver. It thus threatens the successful socialisation of future generations, transmitting to them a culture of crime, despair and dependency.

This scholarly but very readable study is highly original in its combination of economic and sociological analysis. It is also unusual in its scope, covering the United States and countries in Western Europe as diverse as Sweden, the welfare utopia, and Switzerland's minimal welfare system. Nor is it just a critique. Using the Swiss viii			*Preface*

example, the authors propose ways to reform education, health and
social security, to re-invigorate decaying communities, strengthen
the family and, through the encouragement of self-discipline and
independence, produce true welfare – after the welfare state.

The Unit's task is to generate, enliven and inform public debate
on social affairs, and it is with those objectives in mind that I warmly
commend *Cradle to Grave* to the widest possible readership.

Digby Anderson
The Social Affairs Unit
London 1988

Foreword

In the past few years several critical accounts of the welfare state have been published. They have successfully challenged the welfarist assumptions on which social policy in America, Britain, Scandinavia, and many other Western societies has been based for decades (Anderson, 1981; Gilder, 1981, 1986; Seldon, 1981). Building on this critique, this book attempts to take the argument an important stage further.

We have examined the literature of welfare in America, Britain, Scandinavia and the other welfare states systematically. We have conducted interviews with welfare administrators and other key personnel in most of these countries. What we have discovered is that the solutions commonly adopted throughout almost the whole of the Western world to deal with the problems associated with poverty have a high price. They cause more damage and much worse damage than the original problems. Bureaucratic state welfare creates dependency, hurts the poor, inhibits real solutions, and threatens to undermine the foundations of civilised, democratic societies.

One of our major themes is the process by which this damage is done. State welfare, in combination with liberal welfare state policies on divorce and on 'rights' more generally, undermines the family by making fathers redundant. With the family destroyed, its essential role in the socialisation of children goes by the board. In consequence the attitudes and skills required of independent adults in a free society are progressively attenuated. Commitment to self-sufficiency and capacity to achieve and maintain it are sabotaged.

A swelling population of welfare dependents is created. Economically supported outside the labour market, they have little interest in work, and are deprived of the support and discipline which work provides. Inhibited by central state welfare from any real stake in the neighbourhoods in which they live, they watch their local communities decay around them. Educational, health and housing programmes in the inner cities are close to collapse. Employers are frightened off by environmental conditions, by the costs required to maintain what they see as excessive welfare provision, and by the lack of skills and commitment in the demoralised population, and so establish themselves elsewhere. Crime escalates. The life of welfare dependency is institutionalised and normalised, and the fractured family re-creates new generations of children incapable of disciplined and independent lives.

This destructive process is apparent in America, in Britain, in Scandinavia and wherever welfare state policies have been adopted. Unless some radical alternative is found which gets big government off the backs of the people, an increasing proportion of the population will be sucked into welfare dependency. Democratic societies cannot afford the financial costs of state welfare, which drive up taxes, rates and inflation, and squander resources which are needed for productive investment. Still less can the socially destructive effects of excessive state welfare be afforded. Unless these policies are reversed, we are embarked on nothing short of cultural suicide.

THE STRUCTURE OF THE BOOK

The book is in four parts. Part I describes the destructive effects of welfare state policies in the USA, Britain and other countries in Western Europe. We examine education, health, housing, employment and the family. In each case we draw on official statistics, research studies and interviews. In each case the evidence is incontrovertible: welfarist solutions have made social problems in all these areas worse.

We expose the principles underlying such policies as muddled, contradictory and implausible. We reveal how their effect has been to create an ever-expanding sub-class of welfare dependents incapable of supporting democratic freedom or of benefiting from it. We examine the damaging effects of these developments on the economy and culture of free societies.

As a contrast to the deep-seated malaise caused by state welfarism, we turn in Part II to an examination of the exceptional case of Switzerland. On the basis of careful field research we show how the Swiss have managed to avoid overblown state welfare, and in consequence escaped the destructive penalties other Western countries have paid for it.

The Swiss approach insists on individual, family and local responsibility for welfare. It avoids confusing poverty with inequality. It acknowledges the need for effective control of socially damaging deviant behaviour. It presumes that the State's responsibility is to help people towards independence from State support as quickly and as effectively as possible. The result is a free and prosperous society with high levels of social mobility, negligible unemployment and little poverty. The canker of welfare dependency, which elsewhere threatens general prosperity and democratic freedom, is absent.

Part III examines the lessons which comparison of the Swiss case with the welfare states of America, Britain and the rest suggests for countries infected with the welfare virus. We show that Switzerland is not, as is often argued, a special case. Principles, approaches and strategies adopted by the Swiss are entirely compatible with economic, political and cultural conditions in other countries.

All that is required is a decision to reduce welfare provision drastically, and commitment to new policies which solve problems without causing worse ones. Small-scale local communities should have their autonomy, including their financial independence and responsibility, restored. State sabotage of the family should be ended. Redistributive egalitarianism should be abandoned. Help for individuals and families in need should be in the form of loans, temporary, and locally administered. It should be presumed that individuals and families are capable of making arrangements for their own and their dependents' welfare. The power and scale of the central state apparatus should be drastically reduced.

In Part IV the specific implications of our analysis for social policy in Britain and the USA are delineated. Established policy approaches to income maintenance, health, housing, employment and the family are examined. The extent to which these approaches generate welfare dependency, increase poverty, and inhibit any consistent advance towards general prosperity is exposed and criticised.

To answer these weaknesses, radical changes in taxation policy are recommended, together with restoration of more positive attitudes towards the family, education and individual initiative. The dangers of municipal socialism in the conurbations of Britain are also examined, and suggestions made for restoring the power of genuine localism.

The damaging consequences of the welfare policies adopted all over the Western world after the Second World War are now apparent. Governments of left and right alike are reaching around for solutions to the decay and chaos which increasingly characterises all our major cities. Our argument is that nothing less than a reversal of these policies is necessary if we are to avoid a deepening crisis.

The welfare state has proved a damaging distraction and shown itself dangerously counterproductive wherever it has been tried. Instead, we should follow the clue provided by the Swiss, by common sense, and by principles long established in free societies, to reach beyond the welfare state towards real welfare.

Acknowledgements

The authors are indebted to Praeger-Greenwood Press for their permission to use material from the work of Segalman, Ralph, The Swiss Way of Welfare: Lesson for the Western World (New York, 1986) and to the editors of The Public Interest for permission to use material from the article 'Welfare and Dependency in Switzerland', (Winter, 1986) pp. 106–21.

Professor Segalman also wishes to express his deep appreciation to his wife Anita for her help in reading and revising the manuscript.

Part I
The Welfare State in the Western World: American, British and Scandinavian Experience

Part 1

1 Introduction: The Price of Solutions

In the United States there is a metaphoric aphorism, namely, 'Edsel's Law', which states that if a commercial enterprise produces a bad product line (the 'Edsel' of the Ford Motor Company), it soon learns that it has made a mistake. The corollary of the law indicates that if a government establishes a policy which fails, it will probably add to the policy, or build more of such policies, but, in any case, the policy will never be cancelled.

'Edsel's' corollary probably explains why there are so many problems in the welfare states without much discussion of the need to go back to the drawing-board. For what do we find?

High unemployability
High unemployment
High government deficits
A huge body of centralised bureaucracy resistant to cutting
An extensive social pathology in the form of low educational achievement
Increased illegitimacy
Criminality and drug addiction
Extensive alienation
Intermittent riotous behaviour
Emigration of skilled employees

Yet with inflation waiting offstage ready to appear as soon as the temporary recovery is over, most welfare states have lost sight of their goals, and seem to be frantically redoubling their misdirected efforts.

PROBLEMS IN THE WELFARE STATE

Most of the welfare states are beset with large populations of youth and young adults who are generally idle and less than minimally prepared for employment. They seem reluctant even to consider beginning employment which their parents' or grandparents' generation would have taken as a 'first rung' on a lifetime employment ladder. The employment offices, by and large, do not consider these young people as part of the workforce because they are not actively seeking work. For the most part, these young people depend either on the dole and government allowances or on someone else with whom they live, who is also usually a dependent of some government programme. For the most part, these young people live in geographical areas with a high rate of welfare dependency, in subsidised housing which is damaged by years of tenant misuse and mismanagement. The area in which they live often has a high rate of crime, delinquency, drug addiction, alcoholism, violent behaviour, broken families and illegal immigrants. These areas have schools which have a high rate of absenteeism, children who are difficult to control, and a demoralised set of teachers with a high rate of staff turnover. Intact families, especially those with employed heads, either move away from these areas as quickly as they can or they avoid moving into them in the first place.

The dependent population, especially those who live in these areas, have a falling marriage rate, an increasing divorce and desertion rate, and a declining rate of family formation. Children in such areas make up a sizable population. They are a matter for serious concern because they are increasingly being reared in disorganised homes with only one parent. The mother is joined from time to time by intermittent men who are introduced as 'the boyfriend' or 'Uncle John'. Their stay in the home is short in time and they cannot, in any sense, be considered as a father substitute for the children or as a financial or familial support for the mother. The birth rate in such families far outpaces the birth rate of intact, complete families in the population.

THE EFFECTS OF ECONOMIC CHANGES

In addition to these ills, most of the welfare states are suffering a loss of heavy industries to Third-World countries, where unskilled manual labour is cheaper and without the extra employment benefits required by the welfare states. As a result, there is a substantial shift in the employment pattern in the welfare states of those not in government employment. This shift causes a shrinkage of unskilled and 'blue-collar' positions, and the new jobs which do open up have increased requirements of education, job-conditioning, and technical training, often at less pay. Such jobs as do appear are usually located not in the geographical areas of the dependent unemployed, but, in new locations near suburbs and new developments. Moreover, they are concentrated primarily in the service industries. This has already begun in the United States (Eisenstadt, 1985, p. 3), and signs of it have appeared in other welfare states too. This change in future employment patterns causes increased strains on the welfare state. For it represents a cutback of a major population base upon which the welfare states have become increasingly dependent for tax income. The new employment population base will be less well equipped to provide adequate tax income. This new employment pattern is also a matter of serious concern for the future because the replacement birth rate derives from a population which provides inadequate and unsuitable familial socialisation for employment in the new industries.

POLITICAL SUPPORT FOR THE WELFARE STATE

Most of the welfare states have developed extensive programmes of income redistribution which provide substantial grants – euphemistically renamed 'benefits' – despite the fact that they do not require prepayments during prior employment. Many of these grants have been provided because of pressures by groups of proposed beneficiaries. They tend to support the welfare state only to the extent that they continue to benefit. In time, these groups withdraw their political support when proposals are posited to benefit other population groups, or when efforts are made to offset current benefits with increased taxes for such established beneficiaries. Thus, as the welfare state ages, it begins to take on the shape of a gigantic pyramid selling scheme or pyramid swindle – with the older investors benefiting from the support of the newer entries, until, eventually, new support disappears as new entries to the society inherit only guaranteed obligations without benefits. Observers report continued acrimony as each group seeks to maximise its share of command over goods and services.

THE COMPLEX UNCONTROLLABLE WELFARE STATE

Many of the welfare states have also developed an intricate mosaic of social services and welfare income administration. These are both highly centralised and rigidly controlled by a complex of regulations originally installed to protect various political, regional, and/or economic interests involved in the legislative compromises which made possible the policy. Many of these regulations are no longer applicable, or else they have been offset by counter-regulations in later legislation. This has resulted in a maze of requirements satisfied only by a large bureaucracy and private and public lawyers and social workers, whose services are required to keep the constipated system functioning. In France, for example, it is impossible to find one's way through the system without the use of specialised service workers (Fondation pour la Recherche Sociale, 1980).

The colossal bureaucratic centralised funding, adjudication and distribution mechanisms are apparently impervious to electoral and political choices (Eisenstadt, 1985, p. 2). As a result, these pro-grammes have become impersonal, massive in operation, and unable to individualise the services because of the complex of national and regional regulations, and also because of the difficulty of processing decisions through the multiple control complex. For example, in the United States, there are numerous instances where people have been incorrectly reported as deceased, with an unintended stoppage of benefits of over six months. There have also been instances when reports of death of beneficiaries were not processed, with multiple posthumous cheques received by the family of the deceased. With complexity has come a continued burgeoning of staff.

WELFARE AS A RIGHT EQUALS PERMANENT WELFARE FOR MANY

Yet another continuing problem in the welfare states derives from the assumption that welfare is a right, rather than a privilege. A corollary of this assumption is that the beneficiary need do nothing to receive this grant, except to apply and to express (or prove) his neediness. If a claimant gambled away his assets, or even gave them away, it would not make him ineligible. If he refused employment or refused to educate himself for employment or refused to accept training, it would make no difference. He could continue to receive the aid. Any attempts to change the regulations to require him to do otherwise would be doomed, either because of the difficulty of changing the law and regulations, or because of the resistance of the bureaucracy to persuasion.

This conflict between the intent of welfare as a temporary aid (as so understood by most of the public) and welfare as a permanent right (as understood by the welfare bureaucracy and welfare state planners) has serious implications. The welfare state nations, by and large, have given up on the concept of client rehabilitation for self-sufficiency, an intent originally supported by most welfare state proponents. What was to have been a temporary condition has become a permanent cost on the welfare state. As a result, welfare discourages productivity and self-sufficiency and establishes a new mode of approved behaviour in the society – one of acceptance of dependency as the norm.

PRODUCTIVITY AND THE WELFARE STATE

Yet another associated problem of the welfare state is related to productivity. Evidence has accumulated that the welfare state is less productive than the free-enterprise economy. The American experiment in providing a guaranteed minimum income in controlled tests in Seattle and Denver indicated that the guarantee of even a limited income results in sizable reduction in work hours for men and women. Even more damaging consequences of the minimum guaranteed income were indicated in the social realm, with a large percentage of families, particularly among the working poor, being dissolved during their period of subsidy. Thus, helping families with supplementary funds and income guarantees weakens the position of the father in the family to the point where he is actually encouraged to leave. This, in turn, means that the children will not have the socialisation provided by an intact family. These studies also showed that there are psychological and emotional disruptions among those supported under the income guarantee experiment, which were not evident in the control group.

This destructive effect is not limited to the United States. In Sweden, where a guaranteed income has been in force for many decades, and where the pursuit of gender equality has led to abolition of the joint income-tax return, the two-income family is almost mandatory if the couple wishes to stay above the poverty line. Couples seeking to care for their own preschool children are taxed for, but ineligible to receive, benefits such as subsidised meals, which accompany daycare. As a result, marriage among young Swedes is falling, but cohabitation is rising. The Swedish total fertility rate has fallen to 1.5 children per family, despite increases in child allowances (Carlson, 1983).

Thus, among the dependent poor, the working poor and even the middle class, the welfare state has the effect of discouraging the socialisation of children by parents. In its absence, social control becomes difficult and expensive, and the need for a heavily policed state becomes gradually inevitable.

2 Welfare Dependency

Another product of the welfare state experience is the growth of welfare dependency which is transferred from one generation to another. For over 25 years, evidence of this phenomenon was quietly, but firmly, repressed in the United States behind a façade presented by the welfare establishment, the sociological, psychological and economic scholars of poverty, and the social policy formulators. This myth was, for the most part, supported by the media (William Julius Wilson, 1985).

The picture of the welfare-dependent population presented by these people was that the poor were basically all alike. They were supposed to be similar in behaviour to the rest of the population, imbued with the same Protestant ethic and valuing education, work training, employment, self-improvement and self-sufficiency as much as the rest of the population. The behaviour of the poor was supposed to reflect these values.

Indeed, it was claimed by these proponents of the poor that welfare dependency was only temporary in almost all cases, and that the poor would move into self-sufficiency as soon as opportunities became available. In the meantime, all they need is more money to improve their situation.

Their purposes in repressing discussion of the true picture of welfare dependency was no doubt compassionate. Welfare experts, public, academic and journalistic, feared that a contrary view of welfare poverty might lead to more robust management and constraint of welfare, and, perhaps even a revised administration of the policy.

EVIDENCE OF POVERTY

In the meantime, data began to accumulate in the form of Sheehan's *Welfare Mother*, Auletta's *Underclass*, Sharff's *Ghetto Family*, Segalman and Basu's *Poverty in America*, and Murray's *Losing Ground*. In addition, persistent poverty and dependency was reported in England by Townsend, in the Low Countries by Schaber and associates, and others.

In the latter studies, however, the description of the poor tended to define the condition as entirely the results of social factors beyond their own control. It was claimed that it did not in any way derive

9

from individual behaviour, lifestyle or choices. In these European studies, as in the picture of dependent poverty presented in the United States, the poor were depicted as victims of conditions beyond their control, rather than as independent agents who deal with – or choose not to deal with – the problems they encounter.

Two studies made in West Germany by Strang (1970, 1984) found that the poor are not monolithic at all. Some people faced with poverty are able to surmount the problem and can mobilise themselves to do so, while others tend to fall into a life of dependency which persists into subsequent generations. Studies in the United States on residual poverty were numerous, but they persistently claimed that welfare dependency was a myth rather than a fact. In the 1960s, chronic dependency was estimated by scholars and researchers as 'less than 10 per cent'. By the 1970s, they were still reported as insignificant, although the figures indicated about 20 per cent, and this population category represented over 60 per cent of the costs. By the 1980s, they were reported as not a major problem even though some reports indicated a figure of as high as 43 per cent.

In summary, we can conclude that welfare dependency is a major cost to the welfare state, and that the problem can be expected to grow.

DESTRUCTIVE EFFECT OF WELFARE DEPENDENCY

It is important to examine how welfare dependency affects children and society. The Sheehan study, we believe, is typical of the reports of chronic welfare dependency. The Sheehan welfare family had the following characteristics. They are very similar to those reported from other ghetto sources:

(1) a matriarchal pattern of family structure;
(2) many children of different fathers;
(3) childbirth by mother at an early age;
(4) only a tenuous relationship between the family and community, religious organisations, community resources, schools and centres of community services, including employment programmes, and a general fear and suspicion of agencies of community responsibility;
(5) only a tenuous relationship between the immediate family and relatives (particularly male relatives) in the extended family. The only extended family strengths derive from

grandmothers, who were, themselves, reared in a welfare-dependent setting;

(6) a view by the mother which expressed no hope of, or aspirations for, eventually getting her children out of poverty, either by seriously supporting efforts at their education or by encouraging their acquisition or vocational skills;

(7) a child-raising orientation by the mother which lacks authority and purpose, and which is generally disorganised and confused. The mother's control of the children is usually ineffective and episodic, and relies entirely on physical punishments – an option no longer open when the children became physically larger than the mother;

(8) a point of view towards all matters which was fatalistic;

(9) a present-time oriented life pattern which promoted impulsive behaviour, and short attention-span activity, except in the matter of watching hours of television soap opera programmes;

(10) a life history containing a series of poor marriages and/or male liaisons;

(11) behaviour patterns of older children which indicate a continuation of residual welfare dependency. In the case of one daughter, she was already a welfare recipient with her own child, and, in the case of a son, he already had an expensive heroin habit and a history of repeated violations of the law;

(12) a history of missing or unemployed husbands or fathers of the children, each of whom had had only a fluctuating, unclear and temporary place in the family constellation;

(13) a disorganised and impulsively-operated home, with little meal planning and very little organisation of familial duties or clear division of family responsibilities;

(14) a pattern of financial management and credit use which is chaotic and not operated on a basis of purposeful or economic survival priorities;

(15) a relationship with the welfare authorities which is based less on the true facts of the family's situation and more on an attempt to gain maximum financial aid with as little follow-up investigation as possible.

GHETTO DEPENDENCY

Sharff's anthropological study of East Harlem provides a similar family picture. Here, a female-headed matriarchal welfare-dependent family, seemingly without planning to do so, directs its children towards coping models which adjust to welfare dependency and life in the ghetto, rather than towards models related to moving into self-sufficiency and employment. In addition to the 'mother-matriarch', the Sharff family constellation consisted of:

(1) an elder son who is encouraged to free himself from school requirements as early as he can so that he may become the 'street representative' of the family, helping to protect the family from harm by his gang alliances, and helping to supplement the family's disposable income by contributing his street earnings and his share of gang booty. The gang also serves the family in keeping the matriarchal 'boyfriend of the moment' under the matriarch's control. The gang derives its income from various rackets, including 'protection of local merchants', which means that the family is, in part, supported by illegal activity and is tied into a crime syndicate;

(2) a home and childcare manager, a daughter who takes over the care of the younger children and who, in turn and in time, becomes pregnant and brings in her share of welfare support. As in the case of the older son, this child is also encouraged to free herself from school as soon as possible so that she may relieve her mother of home duties;

(3) a family advocate, usually a son, but sometimes a daughter, who alone among all the children is encouraged to stay in school. This is the child who accompanies the mother in all contacts with authorities, whether welfare, school, or police. This child learns to present the family's needs to authorities, to ask for services and benefits, and to protect the family in case of trouble with authorities;

(4) understudies are developed for each of these roles as younger children become available. This is particularly important in the case of the 'street representative', who cannot be expected to be available indefinitely in view of the hazards of gang conflict, delinquency and periodic incarceration. Similarly, as younger girls become available, they learn the roles of welfare motherhood.

It should be noted that these learned roles become instilled in the children and, in time, in *their* children. Their life pattern contains not only a modus vivendi for living in the ghetto, but also a modus vivendi of continued dependency on society. It perpetuates an apartheid condition between the welfare poor and the productive elements of society.

COLLUSION WITH DEPENDENCY

It should be noted that the representatives of mainstream society in contact with welfare families also participate in the perpetuation of the dependency pattern. Examples found in Sheehan's 1976 report include:

(1) provision of money by the welfare agency for moving expenses, which was not used by the family for moving and was never returned by the family, or even requested by the agency;

(2) provision of extra food stamps without checking when the family reported that the first supply was lost. In the process, the client had a double allotment for the period.

(3) acceptance of the client's feeble excuses for not becoming involved in the work-training programme;

(4) the purposeless relationship between the welfare representative and the client, and even a reluctance by the worker to discuss the client's questions on how she might handle her problems;

(5) the systematic separation of social services from eligibility determination provided no opportunity to discuss with the client her continued dependency and the likelihood that her children would follow in her pattern;

(6) the agency's frequent ignoring of obvious lies and manipulations by the client. In several instances this kind of client relationship was rewarded by additional agency grants. The plethora of welfare workers known to the client, all of whom had short and only occasional contacts with her, ensured that the client would not be affected by any relationship with the welfare agency.

The design and structure of the welfare agency is so ineffective in helping the client escape from the welfare trap that it might appear to have been designed by a permanent civil servant in the British television programme 'Yes – Minister'.

3 Education in the Welfare State

A clear connection between the female-headed family to be found in chronic welfare dependency and inadequate educational and school socialisation, inadequate school progress and inadequate preparation of children for necessary purposes of social control has been reported by Dornbusch, *et al*. (1986). Various researchers have tied welfare dependency to hard-core delinquency and have indicated a connection between such families and psychosocial dependency. There are various reports from police agencies that drug addiction is frequently found in broken families and families without suitable fathers. Reports abound from ghetto schools which indicate that only a small proportion of children of broken families are able to complete their education in a satisfactory manner.

THE IMPORTANCE OF EDUCATION

Education is a critical dimension of intergenerational welfare dependency in that it is basic to an individual in preparing for and accepting an occupational role. Without a job he cannot expect to achieve autonomy and a self-sufficient status. Education provides the individual with the necessary verbal and written skills of communication without which work is not possible. Education trains the person for thinking rationally and independently. It provides the learning of social skills and norms necessary for productive interaction with others, and for the acquisition of self-discipline and self-restraint without which learning is impossible.

Education prevents dependency by providing knowledge and skill upon which employment and involvement in the market-place can be built. When it is successfully mastered, education provides substantive human economic capital. It also provides psychological human capital, by strengthening the individual's self-concept and sense of self-worth, and by providing problem-solving skills. The appropriately educated individual knows which doors to knock on, and what to say when they are opened. Because of self-confidence derived from past learning achievements he is ready to risk himself in an encounter with an opportunity. Many less-educated people, because of the low expectations they hold for themselves in mainstream surroundings, tend to avoid such experiences or are lost in making their way in new surroundings.

Education is important in other critical realms of life as well. In health research, for example, it has been found that health conditions of individuals are directly related to the level of education achieved. This correlation can be explained by the role which the individual plays in choices related to his health. The informed patient is all the more likely to be a health-preserving patient. In the absence of knowledge, emotion and myth all too often take control.

RESPONSIBILITY FOR EDUCATION

Most people believe that the main responsibility for education rests on the schools. However, careful examination of the theory and research of learning suggests that it is the early learning years of the child, rather than the school years, which are most critical for successful preparation for later life. Erikson, indicates that every child must successfully surmount a series of struggles, such as trust (versus mistrust), autonomy (versus doubt and shame), initiative (versus guilt), and industry (versus inferiority), during his early years. These mainly precede the usual school experience.

Brown and Madge (1982, p. 97) indicate that family background and experience has an increasing impact over the whole life cycle. The Coleman (1966) and Jencks (1973) studies found a strong basis for concern over family background and experience in relation to successful learning achievement. Bourdieu (1980) and Hinde (1980) demonstrate that the 'cultural capital' provided by parents determines the degree to which educational success, and then occupational success, becomes possible.

FAILURES OF EDUCATION

Careful analysis of the Sheehan (1976) welfare family or the Forman (1982) families in the United States and Britain, and other residual welfare studies in the western nations, indicates that probably the most serious weakness in the welfare-dependent family is its failure to prepare its children for life in the mainstream and for making the most of what schools have to offer for upward mobility.

In the United States, inadequate socialisation of children for schooling has converted ghetto schools from learning centres to behaviour control centres. Desegregation by bussing and other mechanisms has lowered the educational productivity of many American schools, with the result that many middle-class parents (minority and majority) have fled to private, tuition-charging schools, where learning productivity and educational standards are high. Thus, the 'mediocritisation' of American public education has been achieved, a sort of educational redistribution by the welfare state to match its income redistribution goals. This has contributed to the apartheid effect of American income redistribution – a separation of the residual welfare-dependent poor from the self-sufficient society.

In Britain, the early Labour governments supported grammar schools, modern schools and technical schools to match the different talents of students, and to satisfy the variety of preparatory demands of commerce, industry, and universities. Most of these schools have, in recent decades, been replaced by comprehensive schools, which, in the name of democratisation, bundle students with mixed abilities and talents together. These schools usually fail to satisfy the requirements of employers or universities. The homogenisation of schools parallels a similar pattern in the United States.

Both in the United States and Britain, there are private schools with high standards. Private schools are, in both countries, now becoming almost the only entry to better-quality university education and continued upward mobility. With falling standards and educational productivity in the state schools, it is becoming less possible for a student to graduate from a state school and then to enter a prestigious university. Under the new 'egalitarian' system in the state schools, the bright poverty child, who is held back by a class of dullards and misbehaviour-prone children, is outstripped by the dim middle-class or rich boy in the private school. So much for the educational social justice of the welfare state. Middle-class parents soon learn the trick of moving to a neighbourhood where a good state school still functions, despite the high costs of relocating and buying a house in such neighbourhoods. Either that, or they take on extra employment to cover the tuition costs of private schools.

EDUCATIONAL IMPASSE

The educational impasse in public education in the United States and

Britain is not easily resolved. Once the mass of parents in a school district fall behind in appropriate socialisation of their children for learning in the school setting; once they lose (or abdicate) the function of 'policing' their children's learning attitudes and school progress; then the school adopts a defensive position of limited accountability for its progress with the children's learning goals.

Concurrently, as the schools relax their pressure on students and parents for learning achievement, parents and students begin to blame lack of learning progress on the schools and their personnel. When a school or school district begins to fail in its reported and reportable achievements, such as interdistrict exam results, then the funding authorities at all levels make less stringent efforts for teacher salaries, school operational budgets, and so on. In time, teacher and staff morale losses are matched by increased dropout and truancy rates. With the loss of teacher morale comes the disappearance of teacher enthusiasm for teaching and promoting learning.

There is a 'tipping point' in school clienteles and in teacher quality, just as there is in public housing, public hospitals, and other public institutions. As quality of clienteles and staff diminish, and as additional 'difficult students', and/or substitute teachers enter the school, the better students and their parents and the better teachers turn elsewhere. The contemporary problem school district presents similar dynamics to the failing family, in that each partner blames the other for failures which have been created by all of the participants. The solution lies not so much in failure analysis, but in resocialisation of and reimposition of responsibility on parents, children, teachers, and staff. The educational situation provided by the suburban neighbourhood and local school ensures interactive cooperation between parents and teachers, with responsibility, taxing authority, and community accountability resting in local hands. This kind of neighbourhood regulation and structure is sadly anathema to the highly centralised, regulation-ridden bureaucratic welfare state formula for social order.

EDUCATIONAL FAILURE IN SWEDEN

In Sweden the schools have also been affected by welfare-state activity. Because of the high tax rate occasioned by welfare-state services and benefits, both parents are employed in most Swedish families. Thus, Swedish children have less attention from their parents, and school progress has been affected. Reports by Rydenfelt (1981, pp. 41–4) indicate that because of welfare-state legislation, which now restricts the freedom of teachers to control student behaviour, 11 per cent of the teachers in the system left it in 1980, and an additional 22 per cent took early retirement. Twenty per cent of the current teachers are really substitutes, primarily college students. Every tenth teacher in Stockholm was reported to have been beaten, attacked or threatened.

Rydenfelt's report of Swedish schools parallels the frequent reports of violence and vandalism in American schools, where a major part of the cost of the educational system is tied to policing and control procedures unrelated to teaching goals. The ineffectiveness of Swedish schooling is now reflected in increased youth unemployment and unemployability, and a growing population of sex-offenders, alcoholics, drug addicts, and other social outcasts isolated from the mainstream labour market.

ELSEWHERE IN EUROPE

In Holland, the schools have long been 'pillarised', that is, taken over by voluntary or religious sponsorship, but subsidised by government funds. At first, the subsidies were limited to 20 per cent, but by the 1980s these had reached 100 per cent. With full federal payments, school operation has become a matter of negotiation between the centralised voluntary agencies and the government, with parents generally omitted from the equation. Thus, the education of children in the Netherlands Welfare State has become less, rather than more, democratic, and less related to preparation for competence in the market-place (Van Doorn, 1978).

In Denmark (Gress, 1982) the state pays up to 85 per cent of teachers' salaries in the private and independent schools (as compared to 100 per cent in the state schools). Although the schools function reasonably well, Gress notes that there is a loss of commitment and professionalism in the educational establishment, along with an increasing involvement of the schools with political campaigns and group rights. Gress describes the school ethos as one of 'amateurism', a refusal of teachers to teach with authority, an inculcation of anti-business values and a rejection of history. This ethos, Gress reports, has weakened all the public schools in the Scandinavian countries. Even the evening schools or 'second-chance' schools for workers have been politicised to the point where many are now merely centres for the new 'peace movement', and are no longer offering serious substantive learning.

EDUCATIONAL COLLAPSE IN THE USA

A similar malaise has affected many of the public schools in the United States. The Berkeley, California, school system was formerly a bulwark of high educational standards. It coordinated the work of teachers with police and social agency efforts for maximised socialisation of children, even to the point of intervention, in order to improve parental performance and enforcement of community norms, yet, in recent years, it has become involved in an ethos of student freedom and pluralism to the point where truancy is no longer considered a problem by teachers, truant officers or others. Instead of punishment for unauthorised school absences, children are asked to 'rap' with school personnel. The police are no longer involved in the matter and social agencies are no longer associated with the problem of school truancy. An atmosphere of permissiveness and a 'do-your-own-thing' ethos prevails to the point where a serious drug culture pervades the schools (Zellman and Schlossman, 1986).

A similar drug scene is apparent in most American public high schools. Part of the control problem in American schools is the stringent efforts of civil rights advocates (tied to the welfare state) who seek to protect the rights of children for privacy. These rights, however, run counter to the need to search children for drugs and weapons, which is essential if drug and violence problems are to be kept out of the public schools. Until these problems are controlled, little education and child socialisation will be achieved.

4 Health in the Welfare State

In the United States, the Federal government has so far limited itself to Medicare and Medicaid in terms of health service provision. Before the establishment of Medicare in the mid-1960s, medical delivery in the United States still retained a considerable degree of charity work by most physicians, with a heavy involvement of voluntary and philanthropic agencies in the operation of clinics and hospitals. With the introduction of Medicare, which supported a large proportion of medical and hospital costs for the elderly, and which was based on a fee-for-service system to doctors, medical purveyors and hospitals, there was a rapid rise in medical expenditures and medical delivery. Seemingly overnight, with rises in costs and volume, there was a diminution of charity and voluntary medical services.

This increase in prices affected not only Medicare fees (which were social insurance benefits offset by a payroll and member contribution), but also affected the prices of other third-payment services, such as Blue Cross, Blue Shield, and commercial medical insurances. To meet these medical costs, labour unions negotiated for increased medical employee coverage, and this was encouraged by the exemption of such employee benefits from income tax – better to accept a raise in tax-exempt medical care benefits than a wage increase, which would be less than 55c in the dollar after taxes.

On Medicare, there was a partially deductible, limits of service co-payment partially to constrain overutilization, but, on Medicaid, the new programme for welfare beneficiaries and other needy, there was no deductible or limits of service co-payment at all. Under Medicaid, the states would contract to provide payment to physicians, hospitals and other medical purveyors for all services rendered to persons certified as poor or on welfare, and the federal government undertook to underwrite a major portion of these costs. States made individual contracts with the federal government with various service provisions and services based on state programme plans.

CONTROLLING COSTS

The addition of Medicaid spurred an increased impetus to the medical cost inflation rate, which far outran the general inflation rate. The introduction of new technologies and federal funding of additional hospital beds in areas believed to be already amply supplied led to even further medical cost inflation. Finally, medical and hospital costs grew to the point that the federal government began to design methods to restrain costs.

Programmes, such as the establishment of Professional Service Review Organisations, to restrict excessive services, and the Regional Health Service Agencies, to limit authority for unnecessary expansion of health service facilities, were not effective. Nevertheless, they continue to operate and in the process, by their own procedural additions and administrative costs, add to the overhead.

Finally, the federal government established a Diagnostic Group Rate Plan, under which hospitals (and soon doctors) are paid a set amount for each diagnostic category, regardless of time involved in service to the patient. This, in turn, encourages hospitals to discharge patients as soon as possible, and there are complaints from patients who are sent home with no one to provide care for them. The Medicare DGR rates are now being applied to Medicaid rates as well, and other third-party payers (insurance companies, etc.) are adopting the plan in many areas of the United States. With increased limits on amounts and types of care, along with the DGR, welfare clients, who were once overserved in some locations, are now receiving reduced medical services, and what is delivered is unrelated to their specific needs.

There are other mechanisms which are offered to restrain medical inflation without neglect of patients. Health maintenance organisations, such as Kaiser Permanente, have apparently operated effectively in this regard. The HMO provides full care for each patient enrolled, regardless of his condition or medical needs.

HEALTH CARE FOR WELFARE DEPENDENTS

The welfare-dependent, because of his lifestyle, often finds himself lost in the complex of HMO medical services, and has difficulty in following the instructions of medical personnel in the treatment of his problems, in the prevention of medical difficulties and in the building of a healthful lifestyle for himself and his children. The middle class and the working poor, however, usually find themselves well served in HMOs.

Another mechanism to control medical inflation has been encouraged by the Blue Cross and Blue Shield organisations. These are Preferred Provider Organisations, made up of individual general practitioners, specialists and hospitals which agree to provide full medical care for each patient enrolled in the organisation for a set fee. It is too early to determine how effectively these programmes provide high-quality medical care at restricted costs.

In the United States, more than 80 per cent of the population are covered by medical and hospital insurance. It is not too clear how many of those who are not covered are really unemployed and unemployable, and how many are employed in the underground economy (small marginal shops, cocktail waitresses, black-market untaxed services, and illegal enterprises), whose attitude regarding medical and hospital insurance is that they can always be certified for Medicaid if they need it.

It should be noted that the provision of medical care at no cost under Medicaid prevents the development of medical self-sufficiency behaviour among a substantial portion of the American population. Similarly, it is difficult to know how many people during their employable years are impelled to accept employment for fear that they will not be covered by Medicare in their old age. After all, if they haven't worked enough for coverage, they can always be provided with Medicaid as well as Supplementary Security Assistance for the Aged.

THE DRUG PROBLEM

In the United States, yet another problem has occurred in the realm of drug addiction control. A major unit of the Federal government has taken it upon itself to make a study of drug addiction. It undertakes door-to-door sampling, questioning householders on whether or not they use drugs regularly. With increased governmental undercover arrests of drug users, it might seem doubtful that a drug user would admit to the use of drugs. It is not surprising, then, that this federal study reached the conclusion that the drug addiction problem is declining and under control!

Many state and local agencies laugh at the federal study, which is obviously planned to be used as a proof of the administration's effectiveness before the next national election, and a few have likened the study's conclusions to the 'Emperor's Clothes'. Should national policy on something as important as drug addiction be based on an invalid study? Yet none of the local and state authorities and their research, clinical or police personnel are ready to make their questions public for fear that they may make enemies at the central government level and thus miss out on the renewal of their federal grants or their applications for new federal grants. In this way, centralised federal government radically weakens the rational planning and control of health policy and resource distribution.

PROBLEMS WITH THE NHS

In Britain the national health service is almost 40 years old. Health care, at great expense to the economy, is available to all residents without cost, except for minimal fees for particular items. Despite this, observers indicate that there is no evidence that the gap in health standards between socio-economic groups has been narrowing.

One example is that the daughters of blue-collar workers are four times more likely to die before the age of one year than the daughters of managerial and professional classes. For sons, the ratio is five to one. The reason for this disparity is that the deciding factor on mortality rates in industrialised nations (Wilensky, 1975, pp. 95–6) is *not* the availability and quality of health care, but, rather, the cultural life patterns and the health behaviour activity of the affected population. Thus, the manifest function of the welfare-state health service, which is purportedly provided in order to equalise the life chances of all people in the population, is, in reality, not directly related to health care delivery for all.

Just as a 'good' education as an egalitarian goal is not achievable through an intensively funded school system, and education can be improved only by motivation and involvement of the parents, so the most modern and complete health system cannot achieve the egalitarian goal of good health for all without motivation and involvement of the patients.

According to Daniels (1986), nearly ten per cent of the British population is privately insured, and half of these pay for their insurance out of their disposable income. The health care delivery system is ridden with ill-maintained, dirty facilities, with long waits for service, delayed service, inefficient and uncoordinated pro-grammes, low morale among professional and staff workers, and all this despite increasing budgets taking increasing portions from the gross national product.

By and large, there is in Britain a virtual monopoly in the health care system. For those who cannot afford to pay for their own health care, there is only one source – the National Health Service. If its quality is low, there is nowhere else to go for this population. If one has to wait, what alternative is there? Either the patient waits or, worse yet, delays or omits the care, even when it may be vital. In this sense the National Health Service actually prevents people from obtaining the best care available.

NHS AS A MONOPOLISTIC MONSTER

Public criticism from welfare state supporters complains that the very existence of private care (a growing element) draws valuable resources from the public programme. Yet careful analysis of the problems of the public programme forces one to conclude that more money will not solve the problems of the system.

Daniels, in fact, fears that the NHS will become an 'insatiable monster, capable without difficulty of devouring the entire national product', without, of course, delivering good-quality services to all. Daniels is concerned about the attitude of 'democratic masochism', a public attitude towards the health service which requires the patient to *accept* the indignities, delays, impersonality, inefficiency, dilapidation, employee dissatisfaction and staff malaise – a condition similar to the loss of commitment and professionalism identified by Gress in Scandinavian health and school services.

Waugh's (1985) application of the 'Gammon Law of Bureaucratic Displacement' to the National Health Service is appropriate in that increase of expenditures in a bureaucracy will be matched by a fall in production. It is quite possible that with a 24 per cent annual increase of expenditure, the system may fall further in quality and effectiveness, will increasingly be challenged by private medical systems and, finally, will lose the support of the middle and upper income levels of population and become a poor people's health service, but without a means test.

Thus, the charity health programmes for the poor, which were probably quite good in comparison with the current system, and which were eliminated by the National Health Service, will again be available to the poor under the NHS, but without the individualised compassion and professionalism of the earlier time (Green, 1986).

SCANDINAVIAN HEALTH CARE

Health Service in Sweden is also in difficulty. In 1978 the universal health service used 12 per cent of the GNP, and the system is experiencing recurrent emergencies deriving from low productivity, long waiting lists, impersonal treatment of patients, low staff morale, and staff malaise (Rydenfeldt, 1981).

Similar problems have been experienced in other European countries, and, generally, these derive from a basic structural incentive defect, namely, a low level of efficiency and staff interest which extends from the balance sheets to the bed sheets. Having a governmental intermediary somehow removes the invisible controls without which the programme meets no one's standards.

5 Housing in the Welfare State

One of the myths of social work which has been widely adopted by proponents of the welfare state is that the provision of attractive and safe housing will positively affect the behaviour of the poor, and encourage them to adopt a productive, clean, healthful lifestyle, bringing peace and good citizenship to the community.

It was assumed in terms of this myth that residents of subsidised housing would respect such a housing environment, maintain it in pristine condition, and defend it against vandals. For a time, this assumption proved valid, as long as care was taken, in publicly supported housing programmes, to select the tenants from among the working poor, including only families without a record of crime, delinquency, prostitution, unmarried motherhood, child abuse and neglect and drug addiction. This policy of selectivity was installed in housing projects in the early years of their establishment, when philanthropy led the American nation in such enterprises. Planning and managerial staffs were primarily drawn from the private housing field, where tenant selectivity was critical in preventing the bankruptcy of the projects.

The idea of these programmes was to make livable housing possible for limited-income families, who were struggling to improve their lives, exhibiting hard work on the part of the parents, consistent educational effort by the children, and careful housekeeping, home management and budgeting by the mother. Such families were often imbued with the dream of some day owning their own home or, at least, being able to afford rental housing in the private sector. Many of these families did succeed in achieving these goals and were able to improve their economic status as their grown children moved into the society as professional people, educators, civil servants or in other upwardly mobile employment.

CENTRAL STATE INTERVENTION

In the United States, with the onset of the economic depression in the early 1930s, the federal government entered the housing field for the first time, primarily for the purpose – unconnected with housing –

26

of providing jobs and revitalising the economy. It sought to do this in a number of ways. The first method, which can be considered similar to the social insurance approach, consisted of a special mortgage arrangement to make it possible for the working poor and middle-class workers with limited assets, but a regular income from earnings, to buy a house of their own with a small downpayment, an extended mortgage period, and a limited rate of interest.

The mechanism for this was the reinsurance of loans made by banks to approved applicants, so that the banks could offer such loans on more generous terms than if the bank were to be responsible for the risk. The applicant was required to pay a $\frac{1}{2}$ per cent mortgage insurance fee in addition to the interest. This mortgage insurance fee went into a fund which reimbursed banks for any losses they might experience with FHA loans. This system worked effectively for over fifty years, and the mortgage insurance programme actually made a profit.

In addition to this system, parallel loans were set up through the Farm & Home Administration of the Department of Agriculture, the Veteran's Bureau, and special loan programmes were established for home repairs, remodelling and improvements, and for purchase of cooperative apartments and multiple resident ownership of cooperative homes, and so on.

The reasons the home loan system worked so well were twofold: (1) There was a system for discretionary selection of borrowers; and (2) each of the applicants was required to make a downpayment on his loan, which may have been limited in the eyes of the bankers, but was sizable from the point of view of a family with a limited income. This downpayment represented the family's stake in their home, and that, plus the monthly payments they made, which represented, at least in part, their own payment on principal, encouraged the family to care for their property. Over the years, observations of home owners and tenant use of property, when controlled for comparable income, indicate that the home owners not only maintained their property, but saw to it that their children did not vandalise their own or neighbour's homes. Tenants by comparison did far less for their homes. Similarly, home owners were shown to be more concerned about protection of the neighbourhood and were generally more responsible citizens.

A MORE DIRECT METHOD OF INTERVENTION

The second method of providing housing for families with limited income was the mechanism of the federal housing project. In each community, the local authorities passed legislation or ordinances creating a local housing programme board and providing for its election or appointment. This housing board planned a low-cost housing project or a collection of such projects in order to provide housing for families unable to afford to purchase their own homes or to rent adequate housing at commercial rates. The local community or city usually contributed land for the project and the board secured a loan at low interest for the purpose of building the project. These loans were provided by banks or from bonds subsidised and reinsured by the federal government. Because of exemption from city land taxes, because of the government's low interest rates, and because of the provision of only basic facilities within the housing structure (such as the omission of closet doors and so forth), lower rental rates were charged than would have been required in privately owned units.

The fundamental policy for this type of subsidised housing was based on the marginal income of families in most American cities, who were employed, highly employable for the jobs opening up after the depression, and who were rearing children who were attending school regularly – people, that is to say, who were securely on the path towards eventual self-sufficiency. During those years, there were few multi-problem, chronically dependent families. To be admitted into a low-rent housing project, most families had to have at least one employed wage earner and not have any member who had been involved in crime, drugs, alcoholism or other behaviour which might be a problem.

The rentals were set at approximately one-fourth of the family's monthly earnings, and thus the rentals differed for each family. Families were assigned to apartments on the basis of their size, with large families assigned to the larger apartments. Each family was given to understand that the low-rent apartment was theirs only temporarily, and, as soon as their economic situation improved, they would then be expected to move on to the purchase of their own home or to commercial rental housing. Each family was given to understand the rules by which the project would be operated, and families which broke the rules or whose children damaged project property or interfered with other families would be required to leave the project. Management was usually held in the hands of salaried personnel with rental or other business experience.

During the 1930s and 1940s, most of these thousands of projects operated well and without difficulty. Some of the national policymakers and interested academics did object to the lack of tenant advisory councils in many projects, under the assumption that public housing should be operated more on a social relationship rather than a business basis. Where housing advisory councils did exist, some critics of the housing boards complained that the councils lacked leadership because the potential leaders were usually the tenants who had to move from the projects as their economic situations improved. In time, housing board policies permitted over-income families to remain, but at a somewhat increased rental.

TRANSFORMATION OF THE SYSTEM

The nature of the public housing programmes, which provided a needed temporary shelter for the working poor as they moved upwards on the socioeconomic ladder, changed radically with the entry of a number of external forces. The first of these invasions of community autonomy on the housing front was drastically felt in the 1960s and 1970s. The growth of AFDC welfare programmes for millions of children without stable fathers or father surrogates in families led to many families being without suitable housing. These welfare families were homeless not only because of limited income but also because of past damage to rental housing, rental non-payment, and other problems which made them less than attractive to commercial landlords.

Many of these families were being housed in expensive hotel rooms by the local welfare departments. Pressure from the legislators at state and local levels resulted in revision of the public housing selection guidelines which previously limited the percentage of welfare-dependent tenants in the projects. Concurrently, under instigation by neighbourhood legal programmes (funded by the War on Poverty), a number of class action court cases were pressed to ensure the right of prostitutes, ex-criminal offenders, drug addicts, couples without marriage, and unemployables to be granted housing facilities in the project. As the less-desirable and welfare-dependent families moved into the projects, a tipping point was reached, and the upwardly-mobile working-poor families left the projects.

In time, these housing projects became dilapidated and physically dangerous to live in, especially in the high-rise projects, where elevators, doors and stairways were vandalised. Some projects, such as Pruitt-Igoe houses in St Louis, were deserted even by the residual welfare tenants because the project hallways were infested by rats and insects and terrorised by dangerous gangs of children and youth from the families. In time, all tenants moved out, the fixtures were stolen by the gangs, and, eventually, the buildings were demolished and the federal losses were written off.

In other projects, the Pruitt-Igoe fate was averted by training and employing special housing project police forces in large numbers, at great expense. Despite this, most American public housing projects have not been safe places in which to live. In a South Los Angeles project, for example, there is a murderous gang made up of youth and adults who were reared in the project who terrorise the families who live there. It is almost as if the women who entered into a life of welfare dependency and housing project residence have, by their own acts, created their own rapists and muggers. No apartheid area in South Africa can be considered more separate from the normative mainstream population than such a project.

The only successful public housing projects are those in the few cities where federal funds were not accepted and where tenant selection and housing management remained entirely as a prerogative of the local community. In these instances, the projects continued to be a method of serving the transitory poor. Another sector of public housing has succeeded in the specialised programmes serving selected aged and handicapped adults, especially where these were managed by local civic and church groups and provided with federal loan guarantees.

DESTRUCTIVE RENT CONTROL

Still another area of government involvement in housing has had disastrous results. This is particularly evident in New York City, where the colossal megapolis operates a welfare state which is even larger than many nations. Under a 'temporary' measure originally imposed by the federal government in the 1940s, during the Second World War, and extended ever since then by the City of New York, residential housing operates under rent control.

Rents in New York are regulated in two ways. In buildings built before 1947 no increases were allowed until 1969, and many tenants are still paying 1940s prices. In 1969 'rent stabilisation' was applied to all buildings, both those built before 1969, as well as those built later. Only limited increases were permitted for pre-1969 buildings, based on increased operational costs proven by the landlords. Those built after 1969 had rents based on proven landlord costs at the time of opening. Thus, most rents reflect early 1970s costs, despite the multiple inflations which have occurred since then. When a tenant of a rent-controlled apartment moves or dies, the family is often successful in moving in a relative or friend, often collecting a generous amount of 'key money' under the table. If this transfer does not succeed, then the apartment falls out of rent control (1940s prices) and into 'rent stabilisation' (1970s prices). There are also 'vacancy allowances', and other complex regulations which protect sitting tenants and push up rent for newcomers.

Tucker (1986), after careful study, concludes that people who move to New York now pay higher prices than they would have to pay without rent regulations. He reveals that rent control and rent stabilisation primarily protect upper-middle-class people who 'know the ropes' about rental housing and who could easily pay commercial rentals or purchase their own homes or condominiums if rent controls were not in operation. A large proportion of these tenants are participants in the underground economy (artisans who work overtime for cash, couples who are in retail businesses which report only marginal taxes, and so on), and who are reluctant to undergo the credit or tax analysis involved in a housing purchase.

Another factor which perpetuates unnecessary housing bureaucracy is the size of the force of employees of the Department of Housing Preservation and Development, originally established as an enforcement agency, but now operating primarily as tenant advocates before the New York City Housing Courts. Tucker found instances of housing judges and city officials and HPD civil servants (city and state) who also live in bargain rent-controlled apartments and who have a vested interest in perpetuating the system, both in order to preserve their cheap housing deal and to perpetuate their status as high-level civil servants.

The rent-control system in New York has effectively achieved the following conditions:

(1) it has made the building of new housing for the middle class and the working poor so unprofitable that new residential housing has become a rarity;

(2) it has economically discouraged and prevented the maintenance of good housing so that much of it has fallen into an unsafe condition;

(3) it has caused many responsible landlords to sell out to less responsible, 'fly-by-night', 'corporate-ghost-entrepreneurs', who collect all the rent they can and then abandon the properties. These houses then become unsafe and unlivable and are soon abandoned by the tenants and become victim to squatters, vandals and gangs.

(4) it has prevented new capital from entering the housing rehabilitation field because of the concern that such investments will be lost by present and future housing regulations of the city. As a result, New York City has been exempt from the wave of 'gentrification' of inner city housing which has occurred in other cities. As a result, vast areas of the city remain devastated for decades, resembling bombed-out sectors after a major war. These areas become an expense to the city, provide no taxes, and cost large sums in terms of crime control, public health danger and potential for fire hazards;

(5) it has effectively prevented the availability of housing for the poor and near-poor, causing overcrowding and extremely hazardous conditions.

Wherever, throughout Europe, welfare-oriented rent control has been imposed, the same destructive effects have been observed.

6 Employment in the Welfare State

Just as important as family, schooling, and housing in social control is employment. To the extent that welfare, charity, wealth or social insurance make employment unnecessary to the individual in the long or short run, these grants or benefits are desocialising in their effect on individual behaviour.

The achievement of completed training for a job, and the continued acceptance of a person in his job provide a sense of self-worth which equips people for other life endeavours and for retaining a sense of pride in self-sufficiency and in the maintenance of his dependents. The sense of being a productive participant in society promotes the individual's investment in community life, promotion of social order and fulfillment of the norm of reciprocity. It keeps the person in touch with both material and social reality.

Levenstein (1964), in his explanation of *Why People Work*, maintains that 'individuality simply cannot exist without a structured community' in which work and jobs have an important role. Without work, one has no tie to the community except perhaps as a low-valued dependent. Our freedom to be ourselves depends on our work. Work is the process by which one refuses to allow one's life to become a mere vanity.

Pavalko (1971) argues that through work a person gains standing and a place for himself in society. In the modern world, occupational roles are achieved through one's own efforts, rather than inherited, and having an occupational role is proof of one's having made something of oneself. Work thus provides the person with an identity, a set of expectations of how people will interact with him, and with a validated approach to others in society. Without employment, the person is a 'nobody'.

Social indicators reveal that the recently and involuntarily retired have a high mortality rate; the unemployed and the under-employed have a high incidence of mental illness and emotional distress; and the unemployed have a high rate of suicide, divorce, desertion, and separation from mates. Among unemployed and unemployable youth, we find a high incidence of anomy, delinquency, violence, drug addiction, vandalism, and general anti-social behaviour.

UNEMPLOYMENT MEANS LACK OF WORK

In every developed nation except one (Switzerland), there has been chronic unemployment, under-employment, inadequate occupational youth training and high unemployment compensation and related costs.

In the United States, an average of 8 per cent unemployment of the labour force has been consistently reported, without taking into account the millions of discouraged workers and unregistered, outdated workers. Some minorities are reported to have an estimated 16 per cent unemployed, and minority youth have been reported to have a rate which doubles even that.

Those who are employed are themselves in a less than enviable situation, in that in American manufacturing industries, the American family real income has increased only 1 per cent per year over the last 18 years. Conditions in West European nations, Canada, Australia, New Zealand and other developed nations have not been much better. In many of these countries, the minimum wage and restrictive constraints on employers have been maintained and even strengthened, despite studies (such as those reported by Segalman and Basu, pp. 335–42) which indicate that these depress employment, raise production costs, and prevent the availability of employment entry for many young people who end up permanently unemployed, dependent, and frequently part of counter-productive, anti-social activity.

In West Germany, Strang (1970) reports that the productivity problem is tied to the phenomenon of having so many unemployed protected from having to accept a lower status position, if it is offered, that the unemployed remain on unemployment compensation or on the dole longer than is economically appropriate. According to Ferdinand Mount (1986) and others, 'trade union monopoly power' operates to damage employment and economic performance. As a result of these developments, despite the productivity gains of the economy by rationalisation and mechanisation of industry, there has been a great slump in 'smokestack industries' in the older developed countries and a mass exodus of manufacturing to the newer 'miracle-developed' countries where labour is cheap and unregulated and government restraints are generally absent.

DESTROYING EMPLOYMENT

An example of how industry has been beleaguered by government constraint in the developed countries is offered by Roger Starr's *The Rise and Fall of New York City* (1986). In 1946 New York was without doubt the most favoured city in the world. It had profited from the Second World War and was unscarred by it. The city was rich in assets. Its geography served it well. Its harbour was among the best and busiest. It had the finest transportation of any large city. It concentrated millions of workers in the central business district and got them home at night. The city had a high quality of population with almost every talent or skill and a state school system rated among the best. There was a large housing supply and a generally lawful and voluntarily compliant population. The city had a health system foremost in the world, built of public hospitals and clinics buttressed by a network of voluntary and proprietary hospitals and clinics. And best of all, the city had great manufacturing importance, ranking alongside Chicago and Detroit, insuring the city against the risk of depending on a service economy.

What happened to New York? First of all, the manufacturing rampart began to crumble almost immediately, losing 600 000 jobs in ten years. Neighbourhood associations, environmental groups, lawyers, ambitious politicians, and many others joined in the work of moving industry out of their neighbourhoods or the neighbourhoods of their constituents. With the loss of jobs came a loss of work-related transportation. Efforts to economise and rationalise the subways and suburban trains meant cutting out stations and trains, and this was fought against in the name of minority rights. Smaller ridership meant more opportunity for crime, especially violent crime. With this came greater fear among the public and further decreased ridership. Less availability of safe, usable transportation and increased transportation rates have caused factories to move to other locations. Ridership shrank further.

Manufacturing was also affected by housing shortages for employees who could not find or retain housing in a city with Byzantine rent-control regulations. The very rich were not affected – they could pay the price. The very poor were also provided for in public housing. But the middle class, the historic foundation of social order, responsible citizenship and productivity, was so beleagured as to leave the city in droves. This exodus of the middle class was speeded by the desegregation of schools and by enforced bussing, which lowered the educational standards of schools used by the middle class.

AN INFLUX OF WELFARE DEPENDENTS

The subsidy of the welfare-dependent population encouraged an influx of dependent minority families. This, in time, increased the numbers of unemployed and unemployable youth on the streets, and the violent crime and drug addiction rates rose to a point where whole neighbourhoods and public transportation became deserted by the very population elements which ensured social order.

Robert Nisbet (1986) indicates that 'there are no real villains' in this scenario. 'None are needed. The harm that good men do has been ample . . . the eager, pious, nobly-intentioned politicians, administrators, foundation executives and all-purpose intellectuals ready on a moment's notice to spare no effort in coming up with solutions on the grand scale, underwritten by the taxpayers.'

This coalition of 'good men' is, of course, the same destructive element found everywhere in the welfare state acting as futile surrogates for the normative processes of community decision-making.

THE UNEMPLOYMENT BUREAUCRACY

In most of the developed nations, the employment market is serviced by both public and commercial employment placement agencies. Most of the public agencies are funded or subsidised by the central government and are operated by massive civil service rules and regulations, which have had the usual bureaucratising effects. Registration for employment placement or checking for new openings depends primarily on the applicants waiting on long lines, only to be served in a less than effective information exchange. There is no follow-up to check on whether the employment referral was successful, and, if not, on an analysis of why the placement had not occurred. Seldom is the system able to secure 'feedback' so that applicants can be more effectively prepared and referred to employment.

As in all mass programmes, considerable anomy exists, both in the placement bureaucracy and among the applicants. The least socially competent and the least oriented to the employment system and those whose skills are marginal and not in great demand soon fall in to the category of 'discouraged workers'. They who drop out of the labour market and are then subsidised indefinitely by unemployment compensation, disability manipulation (as in Holland), and public welfare. In time, these people and their families become a continuing financial and social cost to the society, often on an intergenerational basis.

The existence of numbers of private commercial employment agencies and their expansive growth in most developed nations is, we believe, an indication of the failure of the welfare state's employment placement system. The success of the commercial agencies can be credited to their greater structural and functional elasticity, the built-in motivation of their staffs to perform competitively, and the necessity to operate productively, without which the agency would die.

YOUTH UNEMPLOYMENT WORSE

The scene among unemployed and unemployable youth is even more serious than among the adult unemployed because it is damaging to society, not only in the here and now, but in the future. Male and female youth unemployment and unemployability has been linked with the growing problem of unmarried motherhood in the United States and Britain. Unemployment and unemployability among youth in all of the developed nations has been tied to growing problems of drug addiction, alcoholism and crime. The growth of female-headed dependent families with children has been tied to problems of non-formation of legitimated families among young people who are unable to support themselves and, nevertheless, produce children whom they cannot adequately socialise. Many of them have been described as a 'no-hope' generation, who, according to Van der Vat (1980), 'lack the incentive to seek work because they came from families' which have accustomed them to the acceptability of unemployment. They leave school too soon, unprepared for the disciplines of work, 'depriving the society of their talents and unwittingly helping to create and enlarge a "bottom of the heap" element.'

Waugh (1985) has concluded that Beveridge was wrong in offering people the welfare option. It may have temporarily arrested the momentary hunger and physical deterioration caused by disease, but it has, by its removal of motivational dynamics, given rise to idleness, ignorance and squalor, the three other giants which Beveridge sought to remove and prevent. Waugh believes that the welfare state has brought about an entirely new dimension of moral deterioration which may make the nation inoperable and indefensible.

7 The Welfare State and the Family

Almost everywhere in the developed nations (again with the possible exception of Switzerland), final eulogies are being written on the passing of the family as an institution. If this were true, it would be a serious matter in the light of the civilising effects of the family in the history of mankind.

What are these civilising effects? There are a number of basic values which are ingrained, both by role example and by didactic indication, in the children of effective families. These include the following.

PLANNING AND WORKING FOR THE FUTURE, RATHER THAN SEEKING IMMEDIATE GRATIFICATION

This includes going to school regularly, doing one's homework, cooperating with the teacher, and using school learning for the purpose of building one's later career. It also includes carefully considering occupational and career choices realistically, undertaking an appropriate training programme at the appropriate time, and completing it; careful examination of employment prospects, and choosing some job, no matter how menial, as long as it offers a beginning step on the employment ladder; and establishing oneself as an honest and sincere employee so that an employer will be ready to provide recommendations for more advanced and remunerative employment.

This may sound like the 'Horatio Alger' legend or a sermon from Samuel Smiles, but it must be noted that those who operate as if the legend were true seem to make more progress than cynical entries in the labour market. This kind of behaviour facilitates the building up on one's personal human capital, even at the expense of immediate comforts and pleasures.

DEVELOPMENT OF A MORAL, SOCIALLY RESPONSIBLE SET OF PERSONAL RULES OF BEHAVIOUR

This means behaving in ways that make trust possible when trust is defined as the reciprocal ability to predict the behaviour of others and oneself and to make choices accordingly. It also involves constantly taking into consideration the perceived wishes and concerns of others, even at some expense to one's own energies and gratifi- cations. This kind of behaviour includes familial and community cooperation and a rejection of attitudes of dependency on others as long as one can care for oneself.

Because trust is a two-way process, this relationship taught to the child by its parents involves expectation of specific behaviours of his parents by the child, as well as expectation of increasingly mature behaviours of the child by his parents. As the circle of the child's world grows, his trust of others and their trust of him grow in parallel. This process defines the child's loyalty and membership in a family, an extended circle of friends and relatives, a neighbourhood, a community, a region, a nation and, ultimately in the human race.

Just as the tie of trusting others and being trusted by others is in a continually dynamic balance, so are the forces of loyalty to and membership in circles of human relationship. Without this reciprocal tie to others and dependence by others on oneself, the consequence is anomie. It is not enough for the person to claim loyalty and love for an undefined and amorphous humanity, as is the case with many disturbed revolutionary or anarchic individuals. The truly civilised person must necessarily retain two-way ties with humanity through direct interaction with others, beginning with a concern for those about him and reaching to all others who are tied to him or her by the human condition.

THE DEVELOPMENT OF BEHAVIOUR WHICH EMPHASISES THINKING OUT THE SOLUTION OF ONE'S PROBLEMS

Rather than resolving problems by evading them or by aggressive confrontation – the primitive 'fight or flight' behaviour exhibited in less civilised populations – civilised behaviour involves self-constraint, rather than self-indulgence, saving more than spending, productivity rather than maximisation of one's pleasures.

It was this complex of behaviour which made the family and the community possible as enduring institutions, and it was these institutions which reinforced appropriate behaviours and thus made the democratic-capitalist market-place and society possible. It is this kind of behaviour which kept masses of the temporary poor during the American depression from becoming permanently dependent, and it is the attenuation of this kind of behaviour which perpetuates welfare dependency which threatens the social order.

THE FAMILY'S INCULCATION OF VALUES

How does a family instil such autonomous, socially-responsible values in a child? It does this by providing the child with two distinct and countervailing dynamic nuclei for his developmental life.

Each of them is equipped by biological, psychological, anatomical and hormonal qualities to perform the necessary services for the child.

The first is a parent whose primary mode of relationship with the child is an ever-ready acceptance of the child and an overriding concern for his or her welfare. This may even reach the point (the child may well believe this) of rejecting all others in her attention to the child. Upon her, at least in the early months, the child can completely depend, and she will support, comfort, provide for, and defend the child with all her energy.

The other countervailing dynamic nucleus of the child's life space is a very different type of parent. This parent's primary mode of relationship with the child is not an ever-ready acceptance of all behaviour. On the contrary this parent seems constantly to test the child. 'What have you learned? 'What have you accomplished?' 'Might you have had better results if you had done thus and so?'

As the child matures, he or she raises the expected level of acceptable behaviour and achievement. In a sense, the first parental model is one upon whom the child depends for protection, nurturing and comfort, and the second parent is one upon whom the child depends for the coaching he requires to enter into autonomy and social responsibility. It is the second parental model who is constantly testing the child and being tested by him who aids the child in learning how he is expected to behave in the world of social reality.

These two models are not always found separately in one or another parent, but, in an effective parenting situation, enough of the qualities of each model exist in a balanced relationship of stability to provide the kind of support and guidance required by the child.

NECESSARY FAMILY RELATIONSHIPS

It should be noted that the child must perceive that despite the differences between the parental models in his life, the path before him is clearly defined by agreement between the two foci of his governance and direction. Here, we need to make a distinction between having a set of interacting and purposive adults in his life versus a collection of non-interacting, unrelated adults. There are many two-parent families where the requisite harmony is missing.

The adults in a child's life must also be perceived as being in firm control of the major parameters of his or her life. If not, the child may see the adult as an 'other' in his life, but not as a *significant* other. Similarly, the parents must be perceived as 'competent' by the child, based on the child's observations of the adult as he or she performs in and out of family, peer and societal situations. If not, the child may 'feel sorry' for the parent, but view him or her as weak and unreliable. The child must also perceive the parent as consistent in his or her demands in terms of constraints, supports and rewards. If this is not the case, the parent is likely to be viewed by the child as manipulable, and therefore of lesser importance in his life space.

Parents of this sort have been described as 'doormats', who can be programmed to provide gratifications on demand, and such adults can hardly be considered 'significant'. The parent, if he/she is to be of significance to the child, must be perceived as primarily rational, a good planner and goal-oriented, especially in his or her concerns for the child. A disorganised parent, unable to control his or her own life space, or unable to postpone his or her own gratifications, will be perceived by the child as less than significant in his life, and an alternative role model will be sought.

The parent must also be perceived by the child as seeking 'success' for the child in the pro-social mainstream. To accomplish this, the parent must be knowledgeable about, familiar with and involved with the societal mainstream, and particularly with the employment and civic market-place. Without this, the child will probably have no avenue of entry into self-sufficient, autonomous, social responsibility.

Again, the parent must be perceived by the child as sufficiently active in and concerned with the child's life and activities. If the greater portion of the child's life and time is spent with servants who have little stake in the child's long-range development, or in day-care, boarding facilities or public institutions, or frequently changed foster homes in which the child has no discernible, consistent and continuing adult figures, then to that extent the parents or surrogate parents become mere portions of an untouchable and unreachable firmament. One cannot shape one's personality around the model of a distant star, or a shifting star, or an intermittent star.

THE NECESSITY FOR TWO PARENTS

Now obviously, no one person can demonstrate all of these qualities full-time. Even if all of these roles could be played by one person, there is neither time nor energy for one person to provide effectively all the necessary models for his or her child. Just as it requires two different humans in collaboration to conceive the child, so it requires at least two different humans to collaborate in shaping him for effective performance in society.

An absent father who is the host on the intermittent excursions permitted under many divorce custody arrangements is insufficient. A stepfather is equally fallible as a parent if his authority is circumscribed and his responsibility is limited. Least of all is the 'mama's boyfriend' of the moment likely to be an effective father. If mama and her 'boyfriend', sharing a household and children, have so little commitment to each other as to avoid marriage, how can the child depend on their even more tenuous commitment to him?

PARENTS COMMITTED TO SOCIETY

Still other requirements have been specified for parents in research reported by Hirschi (1983). He shows that

> if a child is to be reared in a manner which will deter him from force or fraud, the parents must themselves be allied to the values of the social mainstream and of the established marketplace of employment and citizenship. In addition to this, the parents must be in a position to continuously (1) monitor the child's behavior in his interactions with others, (2) recognize deviant behavior when it occurs, and (3) punish such behavior.

The competent parent 'who cares for his child will watch his behaviour, see him doing things he should not do, and correct him'. But, if the parents do not care for the child or do not have the time or energy to monitor the child's behaviour, or if they do not see anything wrong with the child's behaviour, or if they do not have the inclination or means to punish the child, the child is then given the wrong signals and concludes that wrong acts, or unnecessarily dependent acts, or anti-social acts are acts which are either approved of by parents and other social authorities or are at least condoned by society.

According to Hirschi, 'parents of stealers [and other deviant behaviour children] do not track [their children's behaviour], [they] do not interpret stealing [and other anti-social behaviour] as deviant, they do not punish and they do not care'. The surprising finding of these researchers is that child delinquency and crime are caused by both affluence and poverty, in that these two conditions weaken the family's hold on and attention to the child's behaviour, particularly during adolescence.

In a sense, affluence and poverty provide a family with conditions for inadequate, lax or poor child supervision. Among the poor, punishment tends to be 'cheap' on the part of the parent, yelling, screaming, slapping, and hitting, with little or no follow-up, rather than invested with extended parent energy, time, and concern.

CRIME AND THE FAMILY

The single-parent family, these researchers found, is among the most powerful predictors of crime rates. Also children of reconstituted families with step-parents had more crime than children from biological, unbroken families. Involuntarily broken homes, such as by death of a parent had consistently less delinquency than where the home is broken by a parental decision to divorce or separate. The school was also found to be less a factor in delinquency because 'the school can punish only those students who see education as important to them, and many of the delinquent children have never embraced education as a goal, or have given up on it'.

Somewhere, somehow, effective parenting requires not only the ability to teach the child the differences between right and wrong, but also to perceive the multitudinous instances in life where choices must be made. Without these perceptions, the child cannot affect what occurs in his life. Without these, he is equipped with only a kind of learned helplessness by which he will blame everything that has happened to him on 'fate' or 'the system'. The 'poor little me' self-concept will then control his destinies the rest of his life. Only the competent, alert and motivated parent can help him learn to sense the critical crossings in his life when he has to stop, analyse the alternatives, and use caution. This is how the child learns to control what happens to him, to his career, to his marriage, to his health, to his status as a person and citizen, and to his freedom to make decisions in the future. Without this skill in making choices, most children will not be able to enter the mainstream, nor will their children.

The importance of these findings is made clear when one considers that it is inadequately-socialised children – whether from affluent, middle-class, or impoverished families – who enter into delinquent and anti-social behaviour, eventually becoming part of the inner city jungle culture.

When the family as an institution is considered in relation to problems of welfare dependence and social disorganisation it is difficult to determine which comes first – the lack of effective socialisation of children within a complete family, or the prevalence of social pathologies which prevent the adequate formation of effective families.

THE DYNAMICS OF SOCIAL PATHOLOGY

The dynamics of social pathology are generally not well understood. What is clear, however, is that the child without active, effective parenting is more at risk. Unmarried motherhood, alcoholism and drug addiction have been posited, in many instances, as an attempt by a child to fill a void in his or her life. A missing father, a working or otherwise involved mother, may leave the child without the kind of supervised companionship he needs for emotional growth and learning, and thus a 'side track' is chosen by the child for the remainder of his life.

Similarly, the child who chooses gang membership instead of school and job training (or who is pressured into gang membership through the seeming partial or full abdication of his parents) ends up with a choice which may well represent a lasting life pattern. Parental non-involvement, inactivity and abdication is frequently found in families with absent or non-existent fathers, with working mothers, in reconstituted families, and in other units of weakened structure.

The argument that at the least a two-parent family is required for the adequate installation of a super-ego in the child is persuasively made by the Bergers (1984, p. 162). Without it, the child has few behavioural controls, and without these it is impossible for a democracy to persist (p. 172). The Bergers indicate that it is only in the family and community that a competent, responsible personal identity is developed. Without such family socialisation, the product is more animal than human.

The findings of the Bergers on life without the father are supported by Mitscherlich (1970). Without the values provided for the child by the complete family, the very survival of society is threatened. As Durkheim has argued, society's continuance is dependent on a widely-shared moral consensus. Without such common values, the only way a society can be continued is by coercion at all levels.

CHILDREN OF THE WELFARE STATE

It is necessary, at this point, to shift our attention from what children need in the way of values to what the children of the contemporary welfare-state society are provided with. The first family model we need to examine is the welfare-dependent family.

The shattered, welfare-dependent family in the urban ghetto, which we have described in earlier pages, is unable to produce children adequately equipped to re-enter society and the labour market without considerable difficulty and social disturbance. This condition is further aggravated by cultural developments of the past three decades, in consequence of which sizable proportions of the population are likely to lose their capacity for self-sufficient, productive and socially responsible behaviour. This effect is at least in part caused by features of the welfare state.

For example, the availability of welfare has itself contributed to welfare dependency and ghetto social pathology. Either it eliminates the economic function of the father or it provides an economic substitute; with the substitution of the state for the father in the economic process, the father has also been eliminated as a functioning, responsible parent.

This has been reported in so many studies in the Western nations as to make their listing almost superfluous. The welfare state has also served in other ways to weaken the family as an institution. One of them relates to the explosion of civil rights and individual protections which has been promoted in recent years as a function of the welfare state.

THE DANGERS OF 'CIVIL RIGHTS'

The major obstructive effect on the family of the civil liberation movement derives from the relaxation of divorce laws. The 'no-fault' divorce laws are destructive because they provide a right for partners in a marriage to break up without provision for past or future responsibility for the children or for their best interests. This arrangement provides for automatic dissolution of the marriage without in any way ensuring the social and psychological care of the children. Neither does the procedure ensure that the participants in the divorce will learn why their marriage broke up, where the mistakes were made, and what part each partner played in the failure. As a result, neither partner learns from his or her mistakes. Neither do the children gain any lessons from the experiences of their parents, except perhaps how to avoid marriage or how to get out of a marriage so that you can be free to 'do your thing'.

Having made divorce easier by law, we have also made it more acceptable to individuals and the community by the removal of any associated guilt or shame. Couples now make less effort to make their marriages work than they would have otherwise done. After divorce they tend either to avoid marriage or to repeat the same mistakes.

'No-fault' divorce was supposedly enacted to eliminate the rancour of contested divorces, but this has proved false. Instead of contested divorces, we now have prolonged contested resolution of property settlements, child support payments and custody. This sometimes reaches the point where many children from divorces are not responsibly dealt with by their parents, instead becoming pawns or spoiled love objects in a seemingly permanent domestic war.

Some recent data suggest that more than one out of every three children has not seen his or her father in over three years, and the proportion of step-orphans is growing.

IRRESPONSIBLE SEX

The right to divorce at will has been matched by the right of an individual adult to have intercourse with another consenting adult without being answerable to anyone else including the grandparents of children from either the father's or mother's side. These liaisons often are limited to sexual exchanges without too much investigation by either partner of the other's suitability as a potential marriage partner and potential step-parent for the children. Much of the epidemic of child abuse and child neglect stems from the limitations which the children are perceived as setting on the custodial parent's desire for social life.

The removal of legal, social and cultural restraints on sexual intercourse among consenting adults has also contributed to the spread of venereal diseases including the growing epidemic of AIDS. Along with these problems, there has been a growth of drug addiction and related abnormalities in babies caused by the addiction and inadequate self-care among pregnant women. In the past, this was also a concern of the husband, grandparents and other members of the extended family, who have been eliminated from the family by divorce or nonmarriage.

Meanwhile the divorced or absent father, having avoided child support by legal or other means, is free to become someone else's boyfriend, without responsibility, or new husband. Commonly he establishes a new family, which will also be left in time to live on the meagre earnings of a working mother or on public welfare subsistence.

SEXUAL MODELS

The loosening of constraints on sexual intercourse among adults has had further deleterious effects on children. If a child observes that behaviour of this sort is acceptable among divorced parents, it becomes difficult for the divorced parent to teach the children that it is not also acceptable among adolescents. Thus, the familial dissolution explosion has led to an epidemic of sexual intercourse among children. It should be noted that, although sexual intercourse among consenting adults is legally and to some extent, morally acceptable, sexual intercourse by adults with minors is legally described as 'statutory rape'. This is so because intercourse is legally possible only with informed consent, and minors are, by definition, not able to give informed consent. Thus, the legal expansion of sexual rights for adults has led to an explosion of serious criminal behaviour among children, who cannot give informed consent for intercourse and who are not controllable by their parents or society.

GILDER'S VIEWS

George Gilder (1986) has recently written influentially about 'The

Sexual Revolution at Home', in which he describes the effect of the beliefs of Marx, Engels, Women's Liberation and the welfare state on the modern family. He describes the specific roles of mothers and fathers, without which the family cannot function and civilisation begins to falter.

According to Gilder, the mother's role imposes continual challenges, exacting constant alertness and attention, which 'none of the sexual liberators (or welfare-state planners) remotely understand'. With fewer children who remain longer in the household, the focus on each child has increased. He has examined the complaints of women writers about the mother's alleged isolation, her unstimulating environment, her sexual deprivation, her 'entrapment by babies', her boredom, drudgery, and exploitative enslavement by her husband and the capitalist culture. The situation of the American housewife has been proved, according to Gilder's reading of sociological studies, to be different.

These studies suggest that the role of the housewife actually provides the mother with a base for a many-faceted life, which is not tied down to a single organisational structure and a single set of goals, as would be the case if she were employed. Fewer than one-tenth of suburban housewives surveyed report frequent loneliness or boredom. The family and community roles carried on by women could not be assumed by outside agencies. In fact, Gilder believes that 'the woman's role is nothing less than the hub of the human community. Most of the characteristics which we define as humane and individual originate in the mother's love for her children.' Men simply do not have the same deep ties to their children as mothers.

Moreover, according to Gilder, 'the mother assumes charge of the domestic values of the community, its moral, aesthetic, religious, social and sexual concerns', and the success of civilised society depends on how well the women can transmit these values to the men. Thus, the woman and children in the home are the last bastion against the amorality of the technocratic market-place.

Gilder concludes that there is no way to shunt off child care to society, or substantially to reduce its burdens. When children lack the close attention of mothers and the discipline and guidance of fathers, they tend to become barbarians or wastrels who burden or threaten society, rather than do its work. Furthermore, the reports of a number of women researchers are summarised by Gilder to show that motherhood does entail difficult sacrifices of freedom and autonomy, that women are not content with mere influence, power and wealth, and that they are happiest when the female roles of wife and mother are exalted.

THE FATHER'S CRUCIAL ROLE

Gilder also examines the position of the man in relation to the family and society. He argues that it is the man who makes the major sexual sacrifice by renouncing his dream of short-term sexual freedom and self-fulfilment in order to serve a woman and family for a lifetime. The man's propensity for 'the exciting hunt and predatory chase' must be surrendered, just as the woman's destiny as mother requires reining in of her individualistic aspirations. Neither the male nor female role can be shared or relinquished, except at the cost of familial breakdown.

Men who accept the family as destiny cannot support a family on a 40-hour week, so they train at night and on weekends for better-paying jobs or work at two jobs, while saving to enter a small sideline business and performing house repair chores in time they snatch from posited 'leisure time'. They must turn away from alcohol, drugs, extra-curricular sexual opportunities, and other avocations all in support of the provider role. In addition, the family man must pay close attention to the needs and concerns of his wife and children. Other pressures rest on the female as wife and mother.

While a woman at home can remain uncircumscribed and individual in her relationships, the male at work must keep himself replaceable in his earlier years. He must sacrifice his individuality as an obstacle to earnings and settle down to become a functionary defined by a single job, 'a father whose children are earned by his work', and the value of his work is defined by the market-place. The male is likely to succeed in the market-place to the degree that he represses his individual idiosyncrasies, subordinates himself to the narrow limits of his speciality, and avoids the distractions and impulses of his full personality. He has to accept the postion of a 'barbarian of specialisation', an object of his occupational role and career. Men must give over their lives to unrelenting work, day after day, and look ahead to goals in the distant future, struggling with continued fervour against scarcity, chaos and disaster.

By contrast, the man's role which feminists seek is not, according to Gilder, the real role of men at all – it is a fantasy role in a Marxist dream in which 'society' supposedly does all the work.

FEMINIST DELUSIONS

Gilder is concerned by the dangers to the family posed by sexual liberals, who seek to reshape the norms which have ensured that women will perform the indispensable work of the family and induced men to support their families. The welfare state has apparently embraced the feminist vision of the two sexes no longer needing to make the necessary sacrifices to sustain society. Thus, many men are rejecting available jobs and, instead are doing sporadic work, interspersed with vacations on unemployment compensation. Others work episodically in the underground economy, or enjoy the benefits of free (or almost free) board and room 'boyfriend' status with someone else's ex-wife or a welfare client. Many men and women are passing up the marriage rite, remaining on the uncommitted sidelines of childhood and not accepting responsibility for the actions of their adult bodies.

According to Gilder, the pursuit of promiscuous sexual pleasures offered as an alternative to the duties of the family can only lead to misery and despair for the individuals concerned, and social, political and economic anarchy for society. Without a tie to the family, masculine activity can only degenerate into a game. Gilder concludes that the self-sacrifice of women, rooted in the familial 'web of relationships' in the home and community, finds a perfect complement in the self-sacrifice of men within the institution of the family, – self-sacrifice which is essential for effective childrearing.

INDIVIDUAL 'RIGHTS' AND THE NEEDS OF SOCIETY

The welfare state's contemporary emphasis on individual rights has had its most damaging impact on the family. In enforcing the rights of individuals to escape marriage, it has caused the break-up of millions of families. Many of these dissolutions have created single-parent families in which the mother is putatively in charge – but the children no longer listen to their mother, and their father is, to all intents and purposes, completely absent from the scene.

Few fathers contribute to their children's support, and contact with their children tends to be infrequent. The mother now has to support the family, at a lower standard of living and with even less time to devote to the children. Because of her weakened power, lacking reinforcement by the father and paternal relatives, her control of the children's activity is weakened.

School influence on children is effective only as long as the children remain committed to learning and occupational aspirations. But these are tied to school attendance, and this soon disappears in broken families, where children quickly sense an opportunity to 'do their own thing', with parental wishes no longer enforceable.

CHILDREN WITHOUT FAMILIES

The children of such families are in effect parented by their peers, and the moral level of peer-parenting is usually that of the lowest common denominator. The question that needs to be asked is not so much how children are reared for anti-social behaviour as how so many avoid a life on the street. For even the reconstituted family, where divorced parents with children remarry, offers little hope for resolution of the problem. Maggie Gallagher (1986) for example indicates that pre-schoolers in a home with a step-parent are *40 times more likely to be abused* and far more likely to run away than children from homes with two natural parents.

With the father gone and the mother now involved in increased familial responsibilities, in the emotional diversions and handicaps deriving from her renewed single status and with re-entry into the dating and pairing world, the children are likely to have even less contact with their mother. The limited-quality day-care ordinarily available at typical income levels, the problems of finding and balancing a job with family responsibilities and the breakdown of the full family support group, commonly overwhelms the mother altogether.

THE DOMINANCE OF YOUTH CULTURE

The action of the welfare state in making divorce easier, in easing the status of sexual activity without constraints and in permitting and condoning the production of children out of wedlock has had the effect of denigrating the values of sexual fidelity and devotion to familial life. By freeing the family of its father, the welfare state has created an atmosphere which encourages a footloose youth culture and celebrates the pursuit of trivial childish goals throughout life. The right to be 'different', to be oneself, to do what 'feels good', regardless of the consequences to others and without responsibility or consequences for oneself, has had a deleterious effect on the family, on public health and on social order.

RIGHTS WITHOUT RESPONSIBILITIES

In some American states, the right of teenage children to receive an abortion, treatment for venereal disease, or birth control equipment has been upheld even though the child's parents have not been informed, let alone given their consent. In those states – as indeed in Britain and in many European countries – it is illegal for physicians to notify the parents. Thus, ironically the welfare-state ethos still requires parental consent for a child to have her ears pierced or an appendix removed, but not to have an abortion.

This trend toward individual 'rights' is strengthened by the mother's right to leave home (with or without the children), and a child's right to run away without being apprehended or detained. Yet by contrast there are few familial rights for children in a family where one or both parents want to be relieved of their responsibilities. The trend towards the exercise of rights without responsibility is also apparent among young males, who have increasingly adopted aggressive roles beyond parental control. Girls differ only in their stance, which is more frequently passive-aggressive, rather than overtly aggressive.

In American juvenile courts, public defenders are supported by an ethos which insists that neither the parents nor the child is at fault; rather, it is 'the system' which causes juvenile delinquency and crime. Parents are not pressed by the courts for responsible control of children, and they are returned to the streets, where they operate in 'packs'.

PSEUDO-FAMILY CARE

With the breakdown of family and community relations has come a growth in the therapeutic professions and government-supported social services. When people are troubled, it becomes the job of the welfare state to look after them. Originally, the social services were founded on the need to help people solve their problems and to learn better how to function in their families and communities. In time, as the therapeutic professions and social services became more strongly tied to the welfare state and its 'third-party' medical insurance, providers of counselling turned their attention to helping the client 'feel better'. As these professions became more distant from the economic and employment market-place, they lost sight of the goal of guiding their clients back towards life in society.

Until recently, the therapeutic goal was to help the client do better, as a result of which he would then feel better because doing better usually resulted in greater appreciation by others as well as pride in one's achievements. Newer perspectives have shifted the focus to helping the client feel better, regardless apparently of whether or not he did anything to improve his situation. This approach is well suited to the twisted therapeutic philosophy which supposes that all ills derive from society. If anyone has problems, then all that is required is for the 'system' to pay more, or do more for the problem individual.

Along with this viewpoint, the welfare state-cum-civil-rights ethos requires that nothing should be done against the client's wishes. Thus, to press the client to find a job, or train for a job, or to go to school regularly, or to support his family, or to care for her children, or to live by the consequences of his or her choices is somehow supposed to be undemocratic, and an unfair imposition of one's own values on someone else. Of course, this therapeutic stance of helping the client feel better, while not doing better, fits in well with the psychiatric payment method, where the professional is paid by a third-party employer's insurance company, Worker's Compensation programme, or government agency on a fee-for-service basis. To press the client might dissuade him from returning for more help and this is obviously a financially irresponsible act for the practitioner.

THE IMPACT OF SOCIAL WORK

In public and private welfare, social workers, especially in the United States, have tended to follow the lead of the psychiatrists and psychologists, whose status many envied. In their service to public welfare clients these workers had little or no success in rehabilitation of the chronically dependent. Other clients who were not chronically dependent needed little or no help in working out ways to leave the welfare rolls. The Public welfare workers tended to find little purpose in their roles except as agents in the processing of government paper. As the purpose of welfare work became less involved with rehabilitation, although heavily weighted by administrative processes, and as pressure from public sources grew for cutting back on administrative costs, the usual bureaucratic reaction occurred.

Bureaucracies seldom cut back on staff, but the more vacuous or purposeless a bureaucratic job becomes, the more the central office will load workers with informational inquiries to answer public complaints. The additional paperwork is really a futile attempt to tie the chaotic levels of bureaucracy together, to cover the gaps in unanswered and unanswerable questions. This extra paperwork merely adds to the meaningless weight of the job, still further diluting its purpose.

In time the tie between eligibility and social services was broken, removing the unexercised requirement on the client to become rehabilitated or to bring up his or her children in a rehabilitative manner. It also removed the requirement of the eligibility worker to see that the client moved toward self-sufficiency. Helping people become self-sufficient was simply dropped as a goal of the welfare state. Thus, the welfare state has largely succeeded in convincing the public that the role of welfare client is to continue being dependent and that the role of welfare workers and psychotherapy and social service workers is to help the recipients feel better about staying on welfare.

WELFARE APARTHEID

The promotion of a dependent category of population set apart from the taxpayer-independent population has had enormously destructive effects on the community. When apartheid is created by the welfare state machine, the next institution to suffer is the local community. With increased demand for services to keep the economic machine functioning in a situation of dependent populations and populations without adequately internalised social controls, comes increased taxation of the self-supporting population and/or inflation.

With increased demands come increased centralised taxation and increased centralised regulatory mechanisms. With this flow of power to the central government, the local community and local region loses its power. And as the community wanes, it loses it capacity to serve as protector of the local family and neighbourhood. The centrality is unreachable, incompetent, and yields only to narrow, single-issue campaigns, which tend to be expensive and ineffective. Anything the family and community can do, the mass government can do *less* effectively and *more* expensively.

Homeless children roam strange streets under the control of 'loving' pimps, who succeed in directing them where parents have failed. Doorkey children abound in the city. Children wait late at day-care centres for mama's new boyfriend to pick them up – he's a replacement for last year's stepfather. The once healing, cohesive and constraining community and neighbourhood are now without substance and power. We have seen the brave new world, where everyone is provided for and controlled, and we are appalled by it.

8 The Tenets of the Welfare State

We have examined how the welfare state has led the western nations towards the destruction of the institutions and values upon which civilisation and democracy depend. It is important to examine why the planners seek the establishment of a welfare state despite its destructive effects.

Bethell (1985) suggests that 'Western societies are not so much penetrated as infested by people who dream of human nature as-it-might-be. [These people] wield considerable power.' These proponents of the welfare state make a number of unproven assumptions, which they blithely claim to be self-evident. Anyone who dares to question these assumptions is accused either of ignorance or of being an enemy of the poor and the helpless. In fact those who question the value of the welfare state are entirely sincere in their concern for the less affluent. The difference is their belief that the welfare state is ineffective in helping the poor, and damaging to society, as a whole.

These are the assumptions of the welfare state:

Anything that the free enterprise system can do in productivity and skill can also be effectively done by a well-planned welfare state and its civil servants and at no greater costs;

Benefits granted by the welfare state to the population need do no harm to the citizenry, their institutions and their quality of life;

Actions of a welfare state will not cause productive and creative citizens to leave or to want to leave a closed-border society;

Any welfare state can be as efficient and functional as a non-welfare state. This assumption presumes that the bureaucracy of the welfare state will be constrained in its actions and responsive to the needs and interests of the citizenry;

A welfare state can be operated in a manner which is just and fair to all of its citizens;

It is possible for a welfare state to carry out the necessary domestic and international functions of government, and in addition provide economic security for all without inflation, unemployment, or onerous taxation.

MARKETS AND STATES

The facts are that all of these assumptions have been proven invalid. No bureaucratic mechanism, no matter how well equipped with staff and skills, can possibly match the productivity and cost savings of what Adam Smith described as the 'hidden hand' of economics. The competitive market will always, somehow, find a better way to produce saleable goods and services yielding sufficient affluence for many more people than any planner.

The extension of benefits to 'the relatively deprived' cannot be effected, except at the cost of a weakened, costly labour market. Roger Freeman (1981) for example has made it clear that there are severe limits on how far the state can go in transferring huge resources and in redistributing enormous amounts of income without inflicting serious damage on the economy; it produces lowered incentives and efforts, less economic growth, high rates of inflation, tight regulation of people's lives, and intensification of social problems and internal conflicts.

THE ROAD TO SERFDOM AND BACK

The propensity of the welfare state to interfere with the lives of the mass of population in its attempt to manage the market is much greater than the impersonal mechanisms of the market-place. The former is more resented by the population; the latter is either accepted as normative economic process, or else it gives rise to counter-economic action, which usually restores the balance by automatic process. Where the former is bound to be unfair to many, the latter, in the long run, operates in a pattern of fairness for all. Newhouse (1986) has described conditions in Britain and West Germany and suggests that many people take one half of democracy and neglect the other half – they opt for freedom without responsibility. The facts are that responsibility can be learned only in the family; the family can teach it effectively only in a community to which it is responsible; and the community can function effectively only if it is not overwhelmed by the dominance and power of the central government.

Nathan Glazer (1983) has reported that there are increasing pressures both in the United States and in France for decentralisation of social services. This is not only because of the need for administrative efficiency, but because of a growing concern on almost everyone's part about big government and because of disenchantment with distant professionals in the public service.

TOWARDS DE-CENTRALISATION

This reaction has come with the expansion of the self-help movement and local involvement in voluntarism. As education has spread, and as the average citizen has come to see himself as at least the equal of the average social worker, policeman, teacher or civil servant, it was inevitable that he or she would demand a greater role in government. For social services, this meant a taste for less central government and more local government. In Britain too, this shift in attitude from professionalism to self-help has occurred in the housing field, where the view of the public now is that private housing and home ownership are to be preferred on all counts to council tenancy.

In the United States, the shift has been apparent in the left's slogan 'Power to the people', and in the right's pressure for community control of local schools in the suburbs and for decentralisation of large urban school systems. Superintendants of schools no longer stand aloof. They have had to learn to satisfy their citizenry or leave the smaller communities. Physicians are no longer dominant in matters of community health or health-care policy. Social workers are no longer, on the national or local scene, predominant in social policy; their credibility has been almost destroyed by their promotion of a service-dominated solution for welfare reform. There is everywhere at the local level a clamour for professional accountability.

THE NEED FOR FREEDOM

But this is impossible as long as power and real control rests in a distant centrality. The complexity of central government, with its laws, rules and regulations governing every realm of human activity, creates an attitude of confusion and dependency. As the government confuses social insurance and welfare, earnings and taxation, the individual citizen loses track of right and wrong. It would take a savant, rather than a moral hero, to find his way in the legal maze. As a result, the citizen becomes dependent upon a mechanistic, routinised and often, senseless, civil service to understand his duties and rights.

The dependency of the citizen on the bureaucracy has increasingly destructive effects on the economy and confuses parents in their attempts at teaching their children. Right and wrong, under the welfare state, have given way to technical 'black-letter', 'small-print' law to the point where complex, centralised definitions of right and wrong are not well understood, even by the civil service which is supposed to interpret it.

Stan Gebler Davies shows how the more the state cares, the more damage it does. He relates this in particular to public housing, which is not only worse than private housing, but destroys private housing as well. The same goes for public education, public industry, public welfare, public health, public transport and public wealth. The caring, centralised state becomes irresponsible, uncontrollable, bungling, dangerous and unwieldy.

A typical example of the way in which the welfare state operates counter to its manifest purpose occurs in California. Here the welfare state has as one of its purposes the employment of the handicapped. The central government has a large staff of state civil servants involved in vocational rehabilitation offices, vocational education offices, social services and employment placement agencies, scattered all over the state and all centrally responsible to state centralised direction.

Once a year, usually before elections, the Governor's committee for employment of the handicapped holds a huge meeting at a hotel in an urban setting, amid affluent accommodations. State employees all come to the three-day meetings at state expense, including representatives of state agencies with only limited involvement in employment of the handicapped. To this meeting, representatives of key corporations are invited to present their ideas and to hear a replay of all the reasons why the handicapped should be employed, why the handicapped make better employees (they usually want to work), and what the cost benefits of handicapped employment are. After hearing these accounts and pleas (which they have heard many times before), all the participants, having had a good time and a few days off from routine responsibilities, go back to their offices, in which they will again be isolated from other colleagues in similar agencies with the same purpose, and scarcely any additional handicapped will be employed.

Suppose the power, money and control of these agencies were at the local level, and local taxpayers and their representatives were directly concerned with the costs and concerns of the handicapped. Then it would at least be *possible* that vocational educators would really have to work with vocational rehabilitators and employment placement officers for increased employment of the handicapped. But, with power, money and control at the centralised level, the only result of an 'employ-the-handicapped' conference is to make the politicos of the welfare state 'look good'.

PROSTITUTING VOLUNTARISM

Still another way in which the centralised government-cum-welfare state gains control over local communities is by major subventions of local voluntary agencies. Thus, a programme which begins with local volunteer efforts and local policy control and demonstrates local human relationships with its clients is seduced into acceptance of a federal grant. Soon the shape of the local agency is redesigned, its volunteers are now employees following federal rules, and they behave like the impersonal employees of any civil service bureau. The policies of the agency are reshaped to fit federal guidelines (Glazer, 1983) and in time there is no genuine private sector left in the field of welfare policy. Indeed, Rein and Rainwater (1981) maintain that public and voluntary programmes in combination constitute the welfare state society. However, it is the powerful central state apparatus which tends to have the whip hand.

Centralised, over-powerful government makes of the local community a client state with matching bureaucracies to 'interface' with the national administrative forces. With this proliferation of the welfare state, local enterprise and genuine social care are snuffed out.

TOWARDS AN ALTERNATIVE

Patently we cannot continue with an approach which is so thoroughly destructive in its effects. The only feasible alternative is an open, free-enterprise system. But the issue then is whether and how a civilised society so organised can take care of the 'deserving needy' without encouraging them to become 'undeserving'.

How can a society do good without engendering vice? We shall approach this question by considering the unusual case of Switzerland. For there a people seems to have found a way of avoiding the inevitable problems of the welfare states while at the same time providing real care for those in need and genuine welfare for all.

Part II
The Unusual Case of Switzerland

1 Introduction: the Swiss Approach to Poverty

Switzerland is definitely not a welfare state as generally understood. There is, for example, no national health service, and most of the populations are covered by voluntary health insurance. There is no central programme to provide a minimum guaranteed income for all. There is no concept of a right to state support. Nevertheless, it has achieved what nations traditionally defined as welfare states have not: it has successfully avoided welfare dependency and intergenerational poverty, and it has succeeded in this by methods which are strikingly different from those adopted elsewhere. Just *how* Switzerland deals with its poor and shapes its policies to encourage self-sufficiency offers lessons for others which we should not ignore.

The Swiss begin with a view of poverty which is radically different from that in the other developed societies, Their approach to any problem, whatever it is, starts with these questions: 'What needs to be done to change the situation so that the problems will be alleviated, rather than suppressed? What can be done to resolve the problem under consideration, in a way that does not itself bring about unsought results contrary to our purposes?'

Accordingly, the Swiss, in the manner of the highly inventive minds of the industrial revolution, have arrived at a remarkably rational arrangement for the care of the poor, which is strongly utilitarian in approach and intent. This policy is designed to meet two requirements. First to aid the poor in such a way that they would be helped temporarily, without being encouraged to become dependent by the help offered them. Secondly, aid was to be tied to a policy of encouraging the poor to help themselves as much as possible, and moving them as rapidly as possible out of poverty, if not in the current generation, then, at least, in the next.

SWISS SOCIAL INSURANCE AS A PREVENTION OF POVERTY

Still another requirement was to encourage people to provide for their time of need. Most people, unfortunately, are afflicted with what Karen Horney called 'the neurotic exemption', in that, in good times, they never expect to fall into bad circumstances.

Because of this, the Swiss installed a far-ranging and expanding programme of compulsory social insurance. This imposes on each worker and his employer a compulsory shared-risk programme to provide for both expected and unexpected financial needs. Thus, a primarily self-earned insurance programme provides workers with old-age retirement, disability and sickness insurance, survivors' insurance, accident insurance and unemployment compensation.

Unlike the social insurance policies of most other industrialised nations, these programmes are so designed that the beneficiary cannot control the outcome. Unemployment compensation is given only if the person is validly out of work and readily available for employment as it opens up. Disability is strictly defined in such a way that it has not, as in many other nations, become an alternative to work. If a person were to claim a disability, and if he were to work 'on the side', this would soon be revealed in various ways.

In the first place, income tax reports are open to all and the extra income would soon be reported to the social insurance authority. In the second place, neighbours and fellow members of the community would notice this kind of 'double-dipping', and it would soon be reported to the social insurance agency. Finally, there is no underground economy in Switzerland, so it would be impossible to earn an unlisted employment income. If a person were to stay on disability income while training for an athletic event (which did occur in an American city), this would become common knowledge in the Swiss community and would soon be questioned.

GENUINE INSURANCE PRINCIPLES

Social insurance in Switzerland is operated as a true insurance programme, and the only difference between the Swiss programme and the commercial form of insurance is that the Swiss programme covers amost everyone. No commercial insurance company would remain solvent if the clients were allowed to insure themselves against a house fire if they had a hobby of collecting inflammables. Similarly, no social insurance programme can remain viable and generally unsubsidised if the definitions and responsibilities of clients are allowed to be amended after the fact. The lesson which the Swiss have learned from the insurance business generally is that *client behaviour usually changes in relation to administrative actions, unless such changes are subject to control.*

Thus, administrative policy for social insurance has to operate in such a manner as to keep people working and contributing to the fund until a real (not client-fabricated) crisis occurs. Even here, Swiss social insurance requires client rehabilitative activity for the infirm (during the benefit period) so that a return to self-sufficiency will occur if it is possible and feasible. Otherwise, the client care can suffer a lessened benefit.

PREPARING FOR WORK

The emphasis on prevention via social insurance is matched by a heavy emphasis on prevention of dependency via employment preparation. No one in Switzerland, apparently, can avoid efficacious schooling and occupational training. If a child should begin to falter in such preparation for adult self-sufficiency, the whole community becomes concerned – not just the school's personnel, but the whole gamut of formal and informal social control mechanisms become actively involved.

Truancy and dropping out of school before completion is little known in Switzerland, and childen not in school during a school day become the concern of the local youth programmes, the local police, the neighbours, the clergy and anyone else who might be around. Educational-occupational offerings are varied and broad. There are options at every level and far into the adult years, and these are effective.

In Zurich, for example, Swiss males have an educational or apprenticeship completion rate of 97 per cent. Swiss females have a 91 per cent rate, which means that only a small proportion (much smaller than in most developed countries) break off their training in preference for early marriage. Even the resident Italian children of former *Gastarbeiter* have rates of 87 per cent for males and 78 per cent for females, even though many of them experience parental resistance to higher education

The old concept that Switzrland has few resources other than its people is matched by a national policy which ensures that its people are educationally and technologically prepared to take their place in the productive economy.

PREVENTION OF POVERTY BY CONTROL OF IMMIGRATION

Prevention of native poverty is also ensured by strict control of immigration. The Swiss have long realised the limits of their national resources. They hold to the view that they cannot provide for everyone in the world, or even for everyone who would seek to come to Switzerland. They have therefore carefully selected a limited scope of responsibility. These limits, whatever the rest of the world may think of them, begin with a strong concern for 'their own', and with charity to others only after all of their own citizens have been cared for.

While this may seem harsh, it probably produces no worse results than more open-door policies which tend to encourage intergenerational dependency on government aid. In any case, Swiss policy on immigration is stringent, operating almost as if it were controlled by a calibrated spigot, which is opened only when negative unemployment exists, and is quickly shut when Swiss natives begin to draw excessively on unemployment compensation.

2 The Swiss Welfare System

Despite all of this preventative effort, some Swiss do find themselves at times in poverty. Such people are served, not by the federal social insurance programme, but by the local communities and the cantons. The differences between Swiss social insurance and public assistance are carefully maintained because *these differences serve a necessary function*. The social insurances are administered by the central (Federal) government, but public assistance is operated by the local communities and cantons. Social insurance benefits are distributed on the basis of prior coverage during employment, with matched contributions by employee and employer.

SOCIAL INSURANCE

Unlike social insurance policies in other countries, there is no ceiling on social insurance payroll deductions and employer contributions, so that a bank president earning 200 000 Swiss francs per year, and a bank clerk earning 48 000 per year, each pay $4\frac{1}{2}$ per cent into the social insurance fund, namely 9000 and 2160 Swiss francs respectively per annum. This is matched by equal amounts from the employer. But, on retirement, both bank president and bank clerk each receive the same amount in benefits, about 24 000 Swiss francs per annum, or 36 000 per annum if married. This is the benefit from the so-called 'First Pillar', (see below) which is supplemented by much higher benefits from employer retirement funds, which now cover all of the population.

Social insurance benefits are generally much larger than public aid, but seldom at a level equal to full time employment. Thus, social insurance coverage has an attraction to potential workers and yet is not so attractive as to discourage full-time work. Social insurance benefits (unlike public aid) are based on a right on the part of the worker and his family (whether it is for retirement, survivors' support, accident or invalidity support, or unemployment compensation). There is no social stigma attached to acceptance of social insurance benefits, since the employee is merely collecting insurance for which he and his employer have paid.

The benefits are such as to provide for a relatively comfortable survival. Thus, the policy and administration of social insurance in Switzerland is, in many ways, similar to the policies and administration of social insurance in other countries, to the degree that the latter have not been integrated with their public assistance programmes. This is an important proviso.

There is just one exception to the strict separation of social insurance from public assistance. This applies in the case of aged or invalids with an income of less than 12 000 Swiss francs (after deductions of medical costs, excessive rental costs and other special needs). This programme (the *Ergänzungsleistungen*), similar to the Supplementary Security Income programme in the United States, is federally administered, and requires no prior pre-payments.

A limited, but flexible, means test is required, as in all public assistance programmes. The federal government thus provides, in essence, a guaranteed income, on application, for all aged and invalids who are without resources. However the Swiss have wisely avoided setting up such a minimum guaranteed income for employable adults and for families with children. This is because of their concern about the deleterious effect on employment incentives for those who should be self-supporting, and the negative effect on children in families where their role model is an unemployed parent. Thus the income package of social insurance for the aged and infirm consists of a First Pillar (basic earned benefits for old age, disability and survivors), a Second Pillar (a country-wide retirement programme with transferability), additional cantonal social insurances, plus minimum supplementary security income assistance for the aged, sick and handicapped, and individualized welfare programmes for others at the community and cantonal levels.

SWISS PUBLIC ASSISTANCE PROGRAMMES: LOCAL RESPONSIBILITY

Public assistance, unlike social insurance, is not a concern or responsibility of the federal government. By contrast with welfare states, central government is kept out of it entirely. There is not even a federal data-collecting service about public assistance. Control of public assistance by the local community and the cantons has been jealously guarded ever since the creation of the state. Although all individuals have freedom of movement within the country, the individual's home community or canton carries the responsibility of providing for his care, either directly, if the individual is residing there, or on a reimbursement basis for the first five years, if he resides in another community. A person's established place of residence is that community or canton where he has been economically self-sufficient for a specified time, or where he has been aided on a reimbursement basis by another canton for the specified time.

There is an inter-cantonal concordat which prohibits the 'passing on' of any individual or family to another community. This concordat also requires reimbursement by the community of residence to any communities where its residents may move until they become self-sufficient in the new community or until five years have expired.

Because public assistance is funded from local and cantonal sources, it becomes a matter of concern for each local community to prevent public dependency, if possible, and to work with those who are dependent so that they can become self-sufficient as soon as possible. If a family is so beset with problems as to be unable to become self-sufficient in a short space of time, then the community authorities make special efforts to see to it that the children in that family are reared in a manner which will make them self-sufficient as they reach adulthood.

SWISS PUBLIC WELFARE POLICIES

The public welfare programmes of the local communities have a number of policies which they hold in common. Administration of these policies does vary from community to community, but the general effect, in terms of how the welfare workers view their assignments and how they carry them out, is similar.

These policies include the view that all public welfare aid is temporary, and will continue only as long as the cause of impoverishment lasts. Only in the case of the elderly and some of the physically or mentally handicapped, for whom eventual self-help may be ruled out entirely, supplementary public aid may last a lifetime (over and above the national supplementary security aid income described above).

Although the social welfare system is viewed by proponents of the welfare state, as an income-redistribution mechanism, this is not the case with Swiss public welfare. Thus, for the Swiss (other than the handicapped and the aged) any aid plan, once developed individually with the client, is immediately followed by a discussion of how long the aid is to be given, and how soon the client will be able to become self-supporting again.

This kind of a discussion involves questions of education and training completed, past employment and work skills achieved, further education and training required and plans for finding employment again. If full-time employment is not immediately possible, because of child-care arrangements, then school and day-care resources are provided in order to make part-time work possible. Even part-time employment is usually viewed as temporary, in that the client is expected eventually to become fully self-sufficient. There is essentially a 'contract' between the client and the agency which covers the client's and the agency's responsibilities with regard to the amount and manner of service to be given by the agency, and the client's movement toward independence.

The nature of the public aid given in Swiss programmes also differs from that of many other western countries. In Switzerland, it is incumbent on the client to work toward his rehabilitation and toward self-sufficiency. If he does not, his grant can be cut or eliminated. His children also must be reared to become self-sufficient. No such responsibility is placed on the welfare clients of other western nations.

Swiss aid is described in most local community welfare ordinances as 'advice, counselling, information, and other social services, including, if necessary, financial and material aid.' There is usually no uniform schedule of grants, merely a set of guidelines which are considered along with the client's goal and plan. Considerations in calculating the amount of temporary aid include not only the general and special needs of the client, but also the amount of money he can eventually earn, and whether a welfare grant larger than the beginning salary might discourage efforts toward training and employment.

SWISS PATTERNS OF WELFARE ADMINISTRATION

Patterns of welfare administration in Switzerland are radically different from those of other welfare systems. In welfare state societies public welfare is generally given on the basis of equality for each category of clients. The delivery of the welfare grant tends to be seen as the primary purpose of the agency, rather than as merely one of the tools of rehabilitation. Again rehabilitation and social services in other countries are elective, if available at all, and grants are made to clients without any account being taken of the responsibilities of others to help them. Finally welfare grants in other countries remain the same for as long as there are no reports of a change in the client's situation. It can go on indefinitely – and it frequently does. This is not the case in Switzerland, where the amount of the grant is related precisely to the client's progress.

RESPONSIBILITY OF RELATIVES

Another major policy difference between the Swiss and other welfare systems relates to the responsibility of relatives and family. This can extend even to affluent brothers and sisters who are called on to provide aid for needy siblings. Parents and grandparents are always required to provide for their children and grandchildren, if they are able to do so. In the case of grown children in need, parents are called upon to provide aid if they have the resources. Adult children are also required to aid their parents and grandparents if they are in need. Ex-husbands, in cases of divorce (and husbands and fathers in cases of separation), are required to supply adequate spousal and child support.

Where child payments are not forthcoming on a regular basis in such cases, the public welfare agency is required by law to deliver the court-specified sums to the mother and then press for repayment. This system is unlike the American and British experience in that these payments are usually effectively recovered, for a number of reasons which will be discussed later.

THE MEANS TEST

The enforcement of the 'means test' for public welfare in Switzerland is carried out without difficulty. This is facilitated by the tax collection system, which is located in the individual communities. Each year, every person files an income and wealth tax report. Local assessments are first levied on this basis, then cantonal assessments are made, and finally the federal assessments. *For the sum of five francs (exempted in the case of welfare authorities) in most communities, a copy of any individual's tax reports can be secured by anyone and without having to state a reason.* If a report contains inaccuracies, these can be challenged by any other taxpayer. Thus, the tax record is an unusually authentic source for information on a person's resources and economic ability to support himself or his family.

PUBLIC ASSISTANCE AS A LOAN

Public aid, in Swizerland, by contrast with other western countries, can be recovered by the authorities from an adult client or his direct relatives if he later becomes affluent. As a result clients tend to ask for less aid than they would otherwise, because they know that it may have to be reimbursed. Similarly, because public aid funds which are secured under false pretences or by the use of false information can be recovered with interest by the local community, fraud is kept down to a minimum.

CONFIDENTIALITY AND DISCRETION IN RELATIONS BETWEEN WELFARE WORKERS AND CLIENTS

Public welfare is conducted on a confidential basis in Switzerland, as it is in most other western nations. It is illegal under most community ordinances for a public welfare worker to release information without client permission, even if such information is requested by the local public welfare board members. Neither may a public welfare worker interfere with the constitutional or personal rights of a client. This is similar to the public welfare policies of other western nations.

The difference in the Swiss case, however, is that the client is required to co-operate with the welfare worker not only in regard to determination of needs and resources, but also in relation to improving his own situation and that of his family. Thus, a client who does not co-operate in working toward self-sufficiency may find that the nature and extent of his welfare grant has been changed, or that his welfare grant is to be dispersed in small increments by an appointed guardian, or that it is now to be the form of materials and vouchers only. His only recourse is to appeal beyond the worker or supervisor to the public welfare commission or town council. Under these circumstances, the matter of confidentiality becomes moot.

Similarly, the welfare worker is authorised, when necessary, to release information to youth and community authorities *without permission of the client*, where the client has not been acting responsibly and where guardianship is to be considered. Here too, the issue of confidentiality becomes moot.

Swiss public welfare workers and administrators thus exercise considerable discretion in their relationship with clients. This is quite unlike the client-worker relationship in most other western nations, where the interaction is routinised and focused primarily on regulations of eligibility for aid, and the authorised levels of grants. In the Swiss public agency, almost no aspect of the client's life, or that of his family, is prohibited for discussion by the worker.

Unlike the restrictions on public welfare workers in other countries, in Switzerland the worker has generally unlimited controls in requiring interviews with the client, in the terms of collateral visits with the relatives, employers, teachers of the client's children, and others who may, in any way, affect the client's progress toward again becoming independent. Thus the welfare worker can shape, both formally and indirectly as well, the way in which public aid and public social services are used by the client and his family. If a client seeks to go beyond the welfare worker's constraints, or even beyond the agency's constraints, he then comes face to face with community authorities who are almost always in agreement with the goals of client self-reliance. In our interviews with public officials, we learned that they are even more imbued with the need to reduce client dependency than are the welfare workers themselves.

STIGMA

The matter of confidentiality is particularly important in Switzerland because of the issue of 'Stigma'. Welfare in most western countries is somewhat stigmatised by the general public, and this serves to hold down the extent of claims for welfare made by most ordinary people in need. This stigma has the opposite effect, however, on the chronically welfare-dependent, in that it ensures their cultural separation from the world of work and upward mobility.

In Switzerland, where most of the population is 'middle class' in its values and where public welfare dependency has a general air of stigma, there is considerable danger that becoming known as a welfare client may negatively label a person among his friends, neighbours, community and potential employers. Thus, in Switzerland, stigma serves to promote self-sufficiency and client co-operation towards that end.

THE VIEW OF SWISS PUBLIC WELFARE
ADMINISTRATORS

The view of Swiss public welfare administrators towards their clients
seems quite different from that of most public welfare officials in
other western countries. On the causes of poverty, most western
public welfare writings emphasise the circumstances and conditions
of poverty. It is a view which focuses on the structure of society,
unemployment, the lack of attractive low-level employment, the
failings of public education, inadequate vocational training opportunities, and lack of adequate housing opportunities for welfare clientele.

Swiss public welfare writings and discussions by contrast reflect the
view expressed by Heinz Strang (1970) that poverty is often caused
by a variety of factors; these include structural unemployment,
individual problems, and conditions which prevent adequately remunerative employment, as well as dependency. It tends to be presumed
that at least some of these factors may be interactive with the
availability of public aid.

Swiss welfare personnel, unlike their counterparts in other developed countries, tend *to individualise interpretations of why a particular
client is in need.* The major difference between the two views is that
administrators, in the USA, Britain and other societies afflicted with
the welfare state mentality tend to accept welfare need as a *given*,
and to take it for granted that in any modern society there will
always be a sizable proportion of the population in need. Swiss
administrators, on the other hand, tend to view their world as a place
where individuals have a choice, and that if some are in need, this is
because they have made a wrong choice, or because they have been
unfortunate in their circumstances, or because of a combination of
these factors.

WELFARE STATE – OR REAL WELFARE?

What is to be done for and with the poor? Welfare administrators
(in welfare state societies) see the solution as perfectly simple.
Because they define poverty as a lack of money, the way to solve it
is to redistribute some of society's funds to the poor. Swiss welfare
administrators by contrast define poverty as a condition of multiple
causation, and seek to solve the problem by determining the individual
causes in each case and to take steps accordingly.

In a sense, the so-called welfare state deals with poverty as if it were a fated condition, while the Swiss view poverty more rationally, as a problem which needs to be dealt with carefully, according to its precise causes. Western welfare administrators, other than the Swiss, view their clients as 'receivers of benefits', rather than as actors in their own life choices. Swiss administrators view their clients as differentially able to make changes in their lifespace and circumstances once they have been helped to determine what needs to be done.

Welfare state administrators tend to emphasise the goals of efficiency in the 'delivery of benefits', egalitarian handling of clients in a massive system, and improved management of their assignment in the fulfilment of diverse regulations. Under the Swiss system, on the other hand, the emphasis is placed on individual adjustment to society (and to his surroundings) on the part of the client so that he can learn best how to live productively, and to bring his children up as self-sufficient, productive citizens.

The welfare process seems to be seen as a necessary function in the western world, apart from Switzerland, and welfarisation is viewed as inevitable in an imperfect world. In Switzerland, welfarisation is viewed as a process by which people become used to welfare dependency and it is regarded as something to be avoided.

Indeed, many Swiss welfare workers view welfarisation as an iatrogenic disease, *actually caused by professional treatment*. Thus one Swiss welfare official drew a parallel between welfarisation and excessive bed-rest after surgery. '*If the client gets used to inaction, he will lose the ability to fend for himself.*'

3 The Family and Other Limitations on Welfare Dependency

Probably the most effective of the informal controls operating in Switzerland is the family structure. From an early age, Swiss family socialisation, at almost all levels of social stratification, operates to shape children into functional citizens and workers. Community attitudes reinforce the authority of the family over children, and children soon learn that their behaviour must conform to a standard of consideration for others. Each child is impressed with the assignment of picking up after himself, of doing the work assigned to him, and of preparing himself for self-sufficiency. Children soon learn that as members of a family they must care for their siblings and be responsible for their well-being. Because of effective family socialisation, few individuals find themselves in need of community aid.

THE SWISS COMMUNITY

Still another reinforcement of this effect derives from Swiss community planning. After the Second World War, the planning of communities, the location of factories, and the construction of residential development was based on a policy of modern industrialisation without urbanisation. This was not due to national planning, but was the result of strong local initiative and decentralised political power.

Aside from Zurich, which is not a megalopolis when compared with other metropolitan areas in the world, there are few large cities in Switzerland. Most of the population live in small villages and towns, which are easily reached by an effective network of suburban trains, trams and buses. The residents of these towns may work elsewhere, but they participate actively in communal decision-making.

Many communities function on a town-hall basis, and most decisions regarding expenditures, as well as schools, housing and welfare policies, must be ratified either by an election or a meeting of all electors. The social distance in these communities is minimal, and news about individuals travels fast. In this way, people hear about jobs, informal community help is given to the aged and sick, and there is a high level of informal mutual aid.

In such a setting, a considerable degree of neighbourly aid is frequent, as is the operation of numerous voluntary social service programmes. In consequence, public dependency is minimal, and people are more readily helped to settle their problems of employment and economic independence.

In the Swiss community, voluntary activity flourishes, and indeed is expected. All able-bodied men, for example, are required to participate in their volunteer fire department (there are only three professional fire departments). Those who cannot do so, because of their jobs or situation, are permitted to pay a tax instead of serving. There is discussion in some cities of broadening the volunteer service responsibility to other realms of community service. The tax structure and informal, unofficial social control combine to ensure broad participation by almost everyone.

COMMUNITY YOUTH PROGRAMMES AS A CONSTRAINT ON WELFARISATION

Still another pattern of welfare dependency prevention operates out of the community youth authorities in each town. The *Jugendamt*, as it is called, is a publicly supported recreation, social service, supervision and career programme which serves a high proportion of young people in each town. In no other country are such extensive and intensive efforts made to aid and direct a nation's youth into pro-social activities and away from self-destructive and wasteful 'side-tracks'.

The degree and amount of services given to young people and the attempt to tie recreation to character and career development are both effective and unusual. There is a close working relationship between public welfare services and the *Jugendamt* which ensures that families given financial aid are also provided with supervision of their parenting methods when this is appropriate. The ease with which *beistand* (supervision by locally-appointed guardians) is established, and the frequent local emphasis that such services shall include *Rat und Tat* (advice and action) is not matched outside Switzerland.

SWISS DIVORCE COURTS AS WELFARISATION CONSTRAINTS

Still another informal or preventive control of welfarisation can be found in the Swiss divorce courts. Welfarised poverty has become largely feminised in many Western nations, as an aftermath of divorce and unmarried motherhood. These problems are trivial by comparison in Switzerland.

The reason is to be found in the policies and effectiveness of Swiss divorce and family relations courts. In each of the welfare agencies we visited, we found no complaints about divorce courts. On the contrary, we found considerable respect among welfare administrators for their contribution to preventing the growth of welfare. Apparently husbands who are divorced from their families must provide substantial amounts for child and spousal support, and those who do not do so have their wages attached. Funds are advanced automatically to divorced wives with children by the welfare agency, which then secures reimbursement from the fathers by legal mechanisms.

The fact that most fathers do pay what has been specified by the courts makes it more probable that they will also visit their children, and thus serve as a parental influence on them. The only exception to the fulfilment of paternal responsibilities occurs among those few families where the father is a foreigner, so that enforcement of court actions is ineffective. If he leaves the country, the active involvement of the courts in matters of paternity where marriage has not taken place also serves to prevent family dependency. The Swiss rate of paternal determination and paternal support (outside the marriage) is also much higher than in most other nations.

The Swiss rate of children born out of wedlock is reported at 5 per cent in 1982. This has been a relatively static figure (it was 3.8 per cent in 1970) and the effect of this figure is lessened by the fact that over one-third of such births are quickly followed by marriages. In the United States, data in comparison indicate a 1980 figure of 18.4 per cent, and the 1982 estimate is closer to 23 per cent. In contrast to the Swiss pattern, most American out-of-wedlock births are not followed by marriages which would lessen their impact on welfare aid. Similarly, high levels of out-of-wedlock births are found in many other industrialised nations. Probably the low Swiss rate is occasioned by high levels of informal social control, and this has contributed in the pattern of low welfarisation rates. If the father is not available, then the community requires support by the woman, or her parents and siblings.

WHY THE LAW WORKS

Divorce and Family Relations Courts thus have a direct effect on the prevention of female welfarisation. What is less apparent is the frequent informal effect of such court processes. For example a Swiss banker reported in conversation that he had recently provided a bond to guarantee child support. This happened when a divorced man from a small town in Switzerland was summoned to meet the divorce judge. The judge was concerned, not as a judge but as a citizen of the community, that the man's publicly announced betrothal and eventual marriage to a second wife might result in his non-payment of the scheduled child and spousal supports. He did not want to see the community having to support the man's first family, and said that he planned to appear at the impending marriage to protest that this new marriage was fundamentally immoral, in that the man intended to develop a new family at the community's expense. The judge was dissuaded from his plan to protest publicly against the marriage only after the man had posted a bond, participated in by his brothers, sisters, and parents, which guaranteed continued child and spousal support until the children reached maturity.

Most Swiss judges probably do not involve themselves to this extent in the enforcement of their decrees, but this incident provides us with an indication of the informal community controls which serve to limit or prevent welfarisation.

The job of the Divorce and Domestic Relations Courts is eased in many ways by the operation and structure of Swiss society. Each individual votes (elections are frequent as compared with other societies), pays taxes, registers for military duty (up to the age of 55), and may carry out a number of voluntary activities at the offices of his commune (or quarter in the city) where he resides. If he wishes to move to another commune, he must de-register at the offices of the commune where he lives, and then register at the offices of the commune which he is joining. Not to keep one's registry up to date is a violation of tax regulations, compulsory military duty, voting regulations and police regulations. Thus, no errant father can be lost in the system unless he actually leaves Switzerland.

Similarly, the operation of the court system is such that collection of child and spousal support can be enforced by the withholding of wages, by the establishment of liens on property, and by a variety of informal and social constraints. It must also be noted that, by contrast with the practice in many other countries, divorce is not always granted by judges. There is no 'no-fault' divorce in Switzerland, divorces are more difficult to secure, and people work harder to make their marriages work.

SWISS SCHOOLS AS A CONSTRAINT ON WELFARISATION

Unlike the view of education as 'a continuous questioning of the existing world' held by many liberal educators in other western societies, Luscher and his colleagues (1982) found a fundamentally conservative ideology at the base of Swiss education. Under the Swiss model, *'education is seen as a means of integrating children into the "system" and helping them to internalize the norms of the existing order.'*

Schooling is viewed in Switzerland, more than in most other countries, as 'the job of the child'. Just as failure on the job for an adult is more serious in Switzerland, where work has priority over many other activities, so failure in school becomes a matter of concern, not only for the school personnel, but also for the child's family, relatives, family friends, diverse affected agencies, and interested people in the community.

Because of the concern for the family's *'Ruf'* (family reputation in the community), and because in Switzerland more than in many other countries, completion of basic education is the path to economic success and self-sufficiency, parents and children both take the educational process very seriously. Observers of Swiss education have referred to the heavy emphasis placed on scholarship and discipline in Swiss schools, the high status of teachers, and the well-established role obligations and social distance traditionally specified for student–teacher contacts. The Swiss school has few extra-curricular activities and group programmes, and it imposes a heavy academic load.

Integration of children into the system by Swiss schools includes not only academic assignments, but intertwined with these the critically important norms and values of the society. Among these values and norms, a key item is the *'Principle of Subsidiarity'*. Under this principle (according to Luscher, *et al.*): 'Only those tasks which cannot be fulfilled on the initiative of the individual should be taken away from him and given to the community. The same is true of the relationship between smaller groups, such as the canton and the federal state.'

Thus, the family is primary, and after that, the community has priority, and only after that can the canton or federal state make a claim on the loyalty of the individual. Similarly, private and voluntary institutions have priority over state institutions. As a result, loyalty to family and community are instilled early in schoolchildren.

This is accompanied by a concern for the effect of one's behaviour on the rights of others, based not only on the Golden Rule, but also on the concern for what others will think of oneself and one's family. The norms are taught to Swiss schoolchildren, including adherence to local authority, to the consensus, to amicable agreement, and the responsibility of the individual to the group.

VALUES REINFORCED IN PRACTICE

These values are also enforced in the schools. Traditional models of behaviour, respect for and adherence to the wishes of elders, teachers, and parents are all required of Swiss schoolchildren. By contrast with Riesman's model in *The Lonely Crowd*, each child is taught to carry individual responsibility for his actions, whether they occur in groups or alone. Finally, each child has instilled within him the importance of doing his work and of seeking its completion at a level of the highest quality.

Gruner (1982) has indicated that, from early to late age, 'the true Swiss is ready and willing to work, rising early and working late' as if for the joy of it. During interviews with school officials, the same theme was repeated again and again, that Switzerland has no real resources, except for its people. People are valuable to society only to the degree that they are competent, trained and eager to do their best work.

Finally, each child is taught to rely only on himself, or herself, thus providing a lifelong general commitment to economic self-reliance, postponed gratification and conserving one's assets for one's own self-protection. Swiss citizens have one of the highest rates in the world of savings in banks, and one of the highest rates of voluntary health and other insurance, with almost 95% coverage.

Closely tied to the values taught to Swiss children at home and in school is the norm of reciprocity. This essentially states that, in any society, there is 'no free lunch'. It means that people cannot get 'something for nothing', and that if anyone secures something without effort, someone else must have made the effort for him, whether he wanted to or not.

Thus, Swiss children are taught at home and in school that if they are to expect goods and services, they must, in turn, do their work well (which is learning), as well as to carry out the chores assigned to them. Children soon learn that such a *quid pro quo* arrangement amounts to an ethic of not relying on others to do your share of the work. This ethic is reinforced in school, in the community, on the job in the workplace and in the Swiss Army, which embraces all adult able-bodied males.

Because almost all children are adequately socialised for school, and because the Swiss schools are generally effective, its products are not only academically competent, but also fully imbued with the values described above. The Swiss is a self-reliant, work-addicted, proud member of his community, with a secure place in a society which Clinard (1978) observes 'has never had the marked disparities in distribution of wealth that characterises many other European countries. The position of the Swiss worker today is generally more favourable than that of workers in most other countries.' Such an individual could hardly become chronically dependent upon public aid.

EMPLOYMENT AS A CONSTRAINT ON WELFARISATION

More than in most other societies, what an individual does for a living defines him as a person in the Swiss setting. However it is not merely what he does, but how well he does it, that determines the degree of respect he earns from his neighbours and community.

We have already described the importance given to career preparation, vocational training and professional education in Swiss society. Because work is so highly valued people usually seek to perform well at work. Despite the high level of employment, the loss of a valued job can have a devastating effect on a person. The turnover rate for employment is relatively low, and many employees tend to remain in the same job with one firm until retirement. More than in many other countries, the Swiss worker gains social, as well as economic, benefits from his job. Thus, the employment setting serves to keep people from public dependency, not only in a direct sense, but also in terms of influencing their behaviour and performance both at work and away from work.

MILITARY SERVICE AS A WELFARISATION CONSTRAINT

As mentioned above, all adult males in Switzerland are subject to compulsory military service until the age of 55. Every able-bodied young adult is required to spend some months in basic training, followed by annual service in a unit near his home. Employers are required to fund the wages of employees while on military duty, and many companies are glad to do so because military contacts are often helpful and good for business.

If the norms and values of Swiss society and the loyalties of the locality were not fully absorbed by young Swiss males, military service with a local unit will usually complete the process. Each soldier in the Swiss Army is required to operate with a group and is also called upon to do his share within the group and on individual assignments. Thus, Swiss Army experience serves to reinforce those qualities which prevent and operate counter to the welfarisation process. An individual who 'goofs off' at the expense of his unit has to cope with criticism not only during the annual encampment, but in his rifle club where he is required to maintain his shooting record along with other men who know him.

Thus, to request welfare without adequate reason, or to fail to support his wife (or ex-wife) and children, would serve to stigmatise a man in his community. Because a person's reputation in the community is critically important to most Swiss men, it is carefully guarded in terms of appropriate behaviour in the community. Such behaviour is not conducive to welfare dependency.

4 The Extent of Welfare Dependency in Switzerland

We have described the formal and informal constraints on the welfarisation process in Switzerland. Are these constraints effective in limiting welfare dependency? It is important to note that welfare experience over decades indicates that the optimum outcome is achieved by making welfare available adequately for those unable to help themselves, while also controlling it carefully to avoid interference with the labour market.

To constrain welfare too much by formal and informal methods may create hardship for people who have no alternative but to seek it; to make it too freely available, with too few controls, will lead to its spread in the population and over time. This is likely to create problems in the employment market, and other unhappy effects in terms of inflation, immigration and a variety of social ills.

What about the Swiss experience in this regard? Have they been too harsh or too permissive? An examination of the estimated dependency caseload may help to answer the question.

In our search for transgenerational dependency, we sought evidence of dependent welfare in each of the public agencies in the four major localities and one smaller industrial town. In each of these cities and towns, we learned that a major part of the welfare load is made up of what would be described in the United States as the 'medically needy'.

These are people who have insufficient income, either from current earnings or from assets, such as earned social insurance benefits, to be able to meet their basic needs. They include many aged, handicapped, and infirm people. Because there is 95 per cent medical insurance coverage in Switzerland, and because there are some duplications of medical insurance, conservative estimates of those adequately covered for medical care ranges from 78 to 90 per cent. The remainder are provided with medical coverage and reimbursed medical care as needed by their local public welfare agencies. This makes up a sizable amount of the work of the Swiss public welfare agencies, ranging from 20 to 30 per cent of the caseload.

Because there is no central agency to collect information on caseloads, statistics are only available for each locality, and there is no generally uniform statistical format employed in each of the agencies. Thus, we were forced to supplement whatever data was available with estimates gathered from social workers and public welfare officials.

We did not gather data on the temporary caseload, which was made up primarily of people who had used up their unemployment compensation or whose unemployment compensation was less than sufficient to meet immediate survival needs. This group also contained a high proportion who were employed on a part-time basis. In almost all of these cases, the families were intact and were seriously searching for additional employment. Most of the unemployed or partially employed were in areas of industrial recession and were discussing with their social worker possible occupational retraining programmes or moving their families to areas where appropriate employment was becoming available. Many of these families were on the rolls only for continuation of payment of their interim medical insurance and were otherwise self-sufficient.

In all of the agencies visited, we learned that there was a small part of their caseload (aside from the temporary clients, aged, and handicapped, or medically needy), amounting to about 5 to 10 per cent, who represented dependent cases of long duration. These were described in terms which would normally be characterised as multi-problem families.

In each instance, there were such factors as inadequate employment conditioning or training, psychiatric disturbance, a disorganised family life, disorganised handling of family funds, anti-social or incompetent role models for the children, divorced parents, parental neglect of children, distancing of the individuals from their extended families, excessive gambling and so on.

In our analysis of these cases, it appeared that their number was few in proportion to the total welfare load, and that measures were being taken by the public welfare agency either to resolve the dependency in the present generation or to prevent it in the next. We noted that great care was being taken to ensure that children in such multi-problem families were being carefully observed and protected from the destructive life patterns of their parents. In some instances we noted that aid for such families was being maintained only as long as the parents accepted supervision and guidance in relation to their child-rearing patterns. In other instances, we noted that *Beistand* (guardianship or supervision) actions were taken in co-operation with the *Jugendamt* (youth authority) to ensure that parental responsibilities were fulfilled. In still other instances, children were placed in special homes and institutions, where reportedly more than a majority succeeded in maturing into responsible productive citizens.

In discussions of this portion of the public welfare caseload in the agencies we visited, we learned that the use of placement of children in institutions is very much on the decrease. Instead, families with children are currently being given a combination of aid, advice and supervision to ensure that the children are appropriately reared to fit into an employed, self-sufficient population.

In attempting further to identify transgenerational poverty, we sought out the representatives of the *ATD-Vierte Welt* and interviewed the author of a book on poverty in Switzerland (Meyer, 1974). ATD-Vierte Welt representatives estimate that 3 to 5 per cent of the entire Swiss population are transgenerationally dependent. They believe that as unemployment rises, more people fall into structurally-caused poverty and remain there because of an inability to rise from the aided population level.

We questioned this because, at most, the Swiss unemployment rate is not over 3 per cent, and this includes many of the partially unemployed population.

Many of the unemployed are individuals in a family where one or more persons are employed. Thus, it is hard to believe that few of the unemployed ever become self-sufficient again. We learned that the ATD-Vierte Welt organisation had contact with some 2500 Swiss families whom they have hosted in their country-farm vacation programme over the past 15 years. They believe that these families are continually in need.

Both partners in most of these families, they believe, were themselves brought up in poor families. In each of these families at least one of the partners has been or is under *Vormundschaft* (legal supervision), after a period of alcoholism or psychiatric care. Many of the children in these families have been placed in children's institutions or foster homes, usually against the wishes of the parents, but based on their reported inability to provide an appropriate rearing of the children. The parents are said to be unable to find adequately remunerative employment and unable to help their children to use the school and apprenticeship system adequately to become self-sufficient when they reach adulthood. Many of these families have more children than they know how to deal with.

The ability of these families to deal with the realities of everyday life is at best marginal. Some are ex-offenders of the criminal system. They find it impossible to avoid recurring problems or to learn from previous difficulties. They have constant problems of relating to community institutions. Their relations generally are in turmoil. All have problems of *Ruf* (reputation), which makes employment, housing and so on difficult. From the perceptions of these clients, the community and its institutions seemed threatening. Many are the victims or causes of accumulated unpaid debts and instalment payments for items purchased and no longer used.

AN UNDERCLASS?

The Vierte Welt portrayal of these problem families fits the description of *The Welfare Mother* described by Sheehan (1976) and many of *The Underclass* described by Auletta (1982) in the American welfare scene.

Although claims of a larger recurring dependent population were made by the ATD Vierte Welt representatives, it became apparent that in the listing of 2500 families found over 15 years this might be a fair estimate of the number of such families in all of Switzerland. In interviews with the major public welfare agencies, it became clear that no more than at most 3000 to 4000 families in Switzerland are intergenerational multi-problem families.

These multi-problem families can, we believe, be properly designated as 'individual poverty', rather than 'welfare dependent', in the terms of Strang's typology (1970, 1984). Our reason for this conclusion is that there has been little politicisation of the welfare issue in Switzerland, a condition which exists in most of the countries where the welfare clientele and the welfare administration have become symbiotically perpetuative. Similarly, we observed almost no 'bending' of Swiss welfare policies or administrative procedures, but rather a constant and firm adherence to the welfare agency goals of client self-sufficiency.

In a population of approximately 6 500 000, a residual welfare dependency figure of even 4000 represents only 0.06 per cent (less than one-tenth of one per cent). This compares very favourably with the estimates for most other nations.

IS THE SWISS EXAMPLE STABLE?

Our conclusion is that in Switzerland residual public dependency is limited and not welfare-interactive. We have also concluded that this desirable condition prevails because of a combination of interacting factors involving almost full employment, a stable social structure, local responsibility for welfare, a robust and carefully shaped social insurance system, responsible labour and management co-operation, controlled immigration, effective education and apprenticeship programmes, effective youth-serving programmes, effective follow-up of paternal support, welfare policies and cultural reinforcement. We now need to examine the probability that these favourable conditions will continue in the future.

There are a number of strengths in the Swiss situation which portend well for the future in the constraint of prolonged dependency. The continued work interest of the population, as evidenced by the population's work-week referendum and the indication found by Ruth Gurny and associates (1983), that Swiss youth intend to work rather than be maintained by others, lends support to optimism. Recent unrest among young people, as evidenced in 1980, need cause little concern for welfare dependency since these actions were, in general, remarkably responsible when compared with the youth unrest experienced in other countries. Evidence of the responsibility of youth, even in periods of unrest, is provided by the fact that most of them had weapons available to them, but these were not brought into play at all. Events in Britain in 1981 and more recently were far more violent. The levelling off of the divorce rate, the rising age of the newly married, and the current rising rate of marriage all serve to reassure one of the continued restraint of prolonged dependency.

5 Negative Factors

There are a number of other factors, however, which may serve to weaken Switzerland's prevention of prolonged dependency. These include the loosening of family controls as exhibited by the growth of 'coupling' (couples living together without marriage), and the loosening of community involvement of young adults as evidenced by the low rate of voters exercising their franchises in recent elections. The problem of 'coupling' is, of course, offset by the high rate of marriage in this group soon after pregnancy. The problem of apathy among young Swiss voters has been reported to be shrinking as issues of concern to youth have appeared in the elections.

ALCOHOL AND DRUG ABUSE

Of particular concern in relation to the possible growth of chronic dependency are the factors of alcohol and drug abuse. Alcoholism has long been a problem in Switzerland, and it is probably explicable in the light of Swiss social control. For decades, each of the cantons has expended efforts relating to this problem. A special voluntary agency was established to promote non-alcoholic beverages and to educate the public about the dangers of alcohol. The special drug subcommission of the federal government estimates that about 10.5 litres are consumed annually per resident (somewhat over two gallons). This indicates that Switzerland is about tenth in Europe in the overall consumption of alcohol. It is largely concentrated in the male population. The *Swiss Almanac* of the Zurich Sociological Institute indicates that about 26 per cent of the population were heavy drinkers, with the highest consumption between the ages of 25 and 54 years. The alcohol problem was found to surpass the drug abuse problem. The Institute did find that many of the heavy abusers of alcohol and drugs at the age of 19 learn to abstain or to become light- or middle-range consumers of alcohol by the age of 22. Only 26 per cent of the heavy users of alcohol remain heavy users by the age of 22. Similarly, only 23 per cent of the drug abusers remain abusers by that age. It is estimated by Reist and Wagner (1982) that between 130 000 to 140 000 people are serious alcoholics in Switzerland. This is about 2 per cent of the population.

Clinard (1978) reports that 82.2 per cent of the drug cases involved males under the age of 25. He views drug use as a form of protest by some Swiss youth against the more conservative society, much in the same way that some youth will use unusual or bizarre hair and dress stytles to indicate their differences with their elders.

Trimborn (1982) reported that 107 drug-related deaths occurred in Switzerland in 1981, which represents about 1.7 such deaths per 100 000 people. In the United States, the rate is closer to four per 100 000 people. Reist and Wagner's report estimates 13 000 to 15 000 drug abusers in Switzerland. Clinard (1978) believes that 'although these figures may alarm the Swiss, they show far less drug use than in the United States and many other countries.'

For example, in a sample of over 4000 Swiss Army recruits at the age of 22, 77 per cent in 1975 were found never to have used drugs. Follow-up studies on these young men during military service showed little change in the abstinence rate. Victor Reidi of the Berne Youth Authority also believes that drug abuse among a sector of Swiss youth is a form of protest against Swiss conformity and performance requirements. Those who succeed in meeting the society's requirements and standards are less likely to become abusers. In a society such as the United States, non-conformity and inadequate competency would be more easily tolerated. For example, chronic drug and alcohol abusers who are young adults, and who are, thereby considered 'totally disabled', receive a monthly grant in the Supplementary Security Income Program in the United States (in California, the grant is $440.00 per month, tax free, plus medical care). It is as if, in the United States, society, the state, and the federal government had legitimated drug abuse. Reidi views the Swiss situation as more demanding of youth. 'I think there is no country in the world with more rules, more intolerance [of deviance]. Everybody in Bern is a village policeman and in Zurich it is even worse' (or, in some important respects at least, better).

Clinard indicates that the pattern of Swiss drug use rationale by youth is different from that in other societies. In other countries, drug use by youth is often tied to crime, including violent offences. The drug addict will steal, rob or assault others in order to satisfy his habit. Much of the American drug culture is also tied to crime and delinquency. Swiss youth, according to Clinard, use drugs primarily as protest; they will 'generally not steal the property of another as this would harm someone, [but] they believe that their use of drugs is a personal decision.' Thus, the Swiss drug problem is less tied to the drug use patterns experienced elsewhere in the world, where the drug addict has few or no internalised social controls.

However, alcohol and drug abuse problems in Switzerland, while relatively light in comparison with other western nations, are still a serious concern to Swiss policymakers. Although Swiss external controls are probably more effective in detecting and reaching users, and in seeking treatment and rehabilitation for those affected, the problem is growing. The Swiss drug problem is compounded by contagion by visitors and cultures from other lands where drug abuse is more common.

Thus, Swiss youth who have difficulty in conforming to Swiss standards of behaviour and competence are more likely, as time goes on, to learn about the drug culture of young people in other lands, and may see this alternative life pattern as an attractive way of escaping daily pressures. However, as long as Swiss families hold together, as long as Swiss schooling continues to influence youth, as long as the community concerns itself with social problems, and as long as apprenticeships are completed and jobs are secured, it is likely that the vast majority of Swiss youth will continue to conform and perform in the society. The same factors which tend to prevent welfarisation also tend to constrain the alcohol and drug problems.

DIVORCE AND SEPARATION AS COUNTER FACTORS

Yet another potentially negative factor is found in the divorce rate. Divorce often leaves children with only one active parent, and no matter how competent that parent may be, one is usually not enough. This is especially a problem if the custodial parent does not have an adult support group with whom the child and parent can interact (such as the extended family), and if the custodial parent is entirely dependent upon welfare aid. This kind of dependency often locks the parent and child out of adequate contact with others in the social mainstream, and thus provides the children with an incomplete role model.

Where the single parent is employed, the problem is aggravated further because the children are deprived of consistently available parenting in the home, and their role models are often drawn from less than mature leaders in their peer groups. In either instance, although quality day-care facilities do help, there are dangers in terms of inadequate and incomplete socialisation evident in the rearing of children in single-parent families. This, in turn, places such children at risk of encountering problems and becoming dependent during adulthood.

The Swiss have both a low marriage rate and a low divorce rate as compared to other nations. In 1980 and 1981, that rate was 5.6 marriages for every 1000 population. The rate for those same years in the United States was 10.6 per per 1000 population. Swiss divorces in 1981 amounted to a total of 11 131, which calculates at fewer than 1.7 divorces per 1000 population. This compares favourably with the American divorce rate for 1980 of 5.2 divorces per 1000, the Swiss rate being one-third of the American rate. In 1981 there were 311 Swiss divorces per 1000 marriages compared to the American figure of 490 divorces for every 1000 marriages. It may be that the low rate of marriages is due to the greater care and preparation required for a Swiss marriage. In Switzerland, more than in other western countries, marriage is a matter not only for the young couple, but also for agreement or approval by the two extended families. Similarly, Swiss young people are less apt to get married before the groom, at least, is well established economically. Delayed marriage is also a positive factor in restraining the divorce rate, since the people involved are more mature.

What worries the Swiss is that from a total of 4977 divorces in 1965, the number of divorces rose to 11 131 in 1981. These divorces affect almost two children each (1.8 per divorce). However, the number of children living in one-parent homes or step-homes in Switzerland is quite small, namely 20 036 in a population of $6\frac{1}{2}$ million (3 per 1000), as compared to the American figure of approximately one in every three children in the United States (100 times the Swiss rate). It is, nevertheless, a matter of serious concern to the Swiss.

AN OVERVIEW OF THE NEGATIVE FACTORS

An overview of the negative factors we have examined indicates that neither alcohol and drug addiction, nor divorce and separation are of sufficient gravity to lead to increased welfarisation of the population. In general it appears that the Swiss experience in relation to welfarisation can be accepted as a positive exception to experiences in other developed nations, particularly the welfare states.

Observation of other social ills also indicates lower levels in Switzerland than in other western nations. With low inflation, low unemployment, low crime levels, comparatively lower drug and divorce rates, lower school failures, lower unemployability, and lower rates of illegitimacy, it can be concluded that the volume of Swiss social problems is much lower than in other western nations, and yet it provides well for its entire population without the economic debilitation of the welfare state.

Part III
What are the Lessons?

1 Is Switzerland a Special Case?

We have demonstrated that Switzerland has avoided many of the problems of the welfare state. Is that because Switzerland is a special case, a fortunate accident, a small exception? Hardly so, when one considers that Switzerland is as large as, or larger than, many other European nations, including many welfare states, such as Holland, Belgium, and Norway, where welfarisation and its related social ills have become a serious problem.

Another argument might relate to Swiss culture, indicating that Switzerland is so imbued with the religiously-oriented Protestant ethic as to repress welfare dependency. However, one can point to other countries with similar or even stronger Calvinist influences, which have failed the welfarisation and dependency test, among them the Netherlands, Norway and Sweden.

Still another explanation for Switzerland as a special exception might be founded in its historical development. This argument would hold that Switzerland has not yet caught up with the 'ills' of the rest of the industrial world, and that, in time, the Swiss can be counted on to drop their inhibitions against dependency and pride in self-reliance. This argument can be countered by the fact that, apart from some restrained youth protest and some sign of increased 'coupling', there is little other serious evidence of social disorganisation.

The social institutions of Switzerland are intact. There are almost no slums. The social structure is stable. The family is still important. Open adultery is unknown, whereas in many other countries it is condoned. The Swiss work hard, and their children live lives firmly directed toward the goals of self-sufficiency and social responsibility. From these indices, it would be difficult to predict a breakdown of Swiss society, such as is already in evidence in many other countries.

A final argument against accepting the Swiss example relates to Switzerland's alleged homogeneity. The claim is made that Switzerland is composed of a homogeneous population, unlike other nations plagued by welfarisation problems. But is Switzerland really homogeneous? With four different languages, with two major religions, and many schisms appearing within them, with a multiplicity of political parties, and opinions at least equalling the variability existing in many other nations? The answer must be in the negative.

We are forced, therefore, to accept an alternative explanation – namely that Switzerland presents us with an unusual set of welfare policies, reinforced by an effective pattern of schooling, employment and local governmental structures, supported by an involved and concerned population. These add up to an effective instrument for prevention and management of welfare dependency and its associated ills.

2 What Really Makes Switzerland Different?

What does Switzerland have that makes it immune to the problems of the welfare state which we have described in Part I of this book? We have chosen to focus on welfare dependency as one key problem, but careful analysis suggests that welfarisation is only one of a whole complex of inter-related social problems which Switzerland apparently has avoided. It is as if all the Swiss had got together and agreed to do everything possible to make their members maximally productive.

What are the norms, values and methods by which Switzerland has achieved this success? First we should note that Switzerland's constitution was modelled after that of the USA as it was originally. Thus Switzerland is a confederation of states, as was the USA at first. When difficulties between the autonomous states arose, the Americans chose to revise their country into a central Federalist model. In America, the federal government limits the legal and taxing rights of the states. Hardly anything of importance is undertaken by the states or localities unless they have the approval and support of the federal government. Power has shifted to the central government on almost every conceivable issue. The same centralised power model exists in almost every other western nation, including Britain, France and Scandinavia.

The result is that local and state government has less status and power and fewer able people are drawn to these levels of government to make them effective. On the other hand, attempts at influencing central government by local people are very difficult. Regional and local government policies are, to a great extent, results of centralised decision-making. By and large, except for periods of crisis, most communities do not try to solve their own problems, and could not do so if they tried, except by appeals to the central government. In many of the larger cities an aura of apathy prevails. Even where a city or town operates an effective government, it is often because its leaders have influence in the capital.

The general picture in the western nations is one of huge social, fiscal and governmental problems, problems which cannot be resolved by the participation of its local citizens, and eventually become unmanageable, even with the involvement of the best minds and leaders. A general apathy pervades most local and regional capitals.

ACTIVE LOCALISM

The Swiss scene is very different. Recognition of problems is first made at local level. If the problem cannot be resolved at a strictly local level, then representatives of other nearby localities who may be affected by the same problem are consulted. Most area problems are resolved by inter-communal compacts.

A group of towns in the Swiss hinterland, for example, considered the problem of how to develop a multi-service centre to deal with multi-problem families. The costs could not be borne by one community alone, but by the writing of an inter-communal compact the multi-service agency became the responsibility of the four communities together.

In general, the atmosphere in Swiss towns seems very different from the towns of other countries. Swiss people seem proud of their towns and almost all the citizenry are involved in their operations.

LOCAL LEADERSHIP

In many other western nations, there is often a sense of distrust of the local leader, as if he represents the lowest level of goodwill for the unfortunate; as if his only interest is in tax savings or in political one-upmanship, and as if he were the least informed among those involved in social planning. In Switzerland by contrast, the best informed people are elected to local government, and it is usually the least corrupt and most concerned who become the local leaders.

Again, the pathway to local leadership is comparatively open in the Swiss community. Because everyone is watching everyone on the local scene, and because accounts are legally open, there is very little fraud. In an interview with Professor Hans Tschudi, former president of Switzerland, we learned that he had got his start in Swiss politics by working as a commissioner in the Basle Town community on their Buildings and Works Programme. *In over 20 years of service on this commission, not one instance of fraud was reported.*

Apparently, only at the local level is it possible for everyone to know each other. It is also possible at this level to ask relevant questions and to receive clear answers. It is possible at the local level to understand the issues and the people affected. And, at the local level, the citizen either gets involved in the issues or, if he does not, he has to suffer with the results of someone else's activity.

LEGAL POWERS

Another basic difference between Switzerland and other western nations relates to the power of the federal legislature and the federal courts. On the Swiss scene, the federal courts have never entered into the question of the validity or invalidity of legislative or executive actions. The Swiss federal courts serve only as a final arbiter in individual conflicts, but do not enter into the creation of law by class action decisions. That, the Swiss believe, is the job of the legislatures and, in the last analysis, it is up to the voters either by referendum or initiative.

The Swiss federal court does not permeate into the localities and courts. Thus, a community or canton may act in accordance with the will of its voters, and as long as it does not interfere with other communes or cantons, it may continue this policy despite the fact that its actions do not parallel those of other communities and cantons.

Local autonomy is based on local financing and on local responsibility. Swiss legislation always has a central test question asked before it is submitted to the voters for approval. *Does this law grant rights for something without holding the beneficiary responsible for his actions? Does this law hold someone responsible for some act or behaviour without matching that responsibility with its related rights?*

The Swiss, by long experience, have learned that to grant rights without responsibility or to require responsibility without commensurate rights will only end with unanticipated, distorted and counterproductive consequences in the behaviour of the affected persons.

RIGHTS AND RESPONSIBILITIES

Thus, the grant of public welfare requires certain responses on the part of the client which will limit the extent and duration of public aid benefits. For each of the rights or benefits granted, there is an established *quid pro quo* to be performed.

Moreover Swiss elected officials at all levels of government are closely attuned to the complex of Swiss ethics, involving honesty, self-reliance, hard work, the norm of reciprocity, local control and family responsibility. No law or regulation is passed which may, in any way, operate counter to the above ethics, except in the instance of the aged or sick who cannot, for the present, fend for themselves.

Even in these instances, the government seeks to use private programmes of aid if possible, and great care is exerted to prevent federal or cantonal intrusions into local affairs. For example, the problem of 'concubinage' (persons living together without marriage) was seriously considered by all levels of government because it poses a possible threat to family life and adequate child socialisation. But, after much discussion, it was left to the cantons to act, and in seven cantons, the practice is still illegal.

The Swiss have learned that culture can operate counter to the law, in which case the law becomes vacuous, or the ethic is weakened. Culture can also operate to support the law, in which case the law is strengthened and the society remains stable. This latter is apparently the fortunate condition of Switzerland. Had the Swiss society passed laws which operated counter to the prevalent ethic, counter-productive social change might well have occurred, and Switzerland would today be faced with many problems which are common elsewhere.

ORGANISING WELFARE

In making a comparison between the Swiss model of social control and social welfare and the welfare state models of other nations, a number of hypotheses can be offered. The larger the system or programme of social welfare or social control, the greater the disparity between the intended purpose of the programme and the actual effect; the more likely it is that some people for whom benefits were intended will not be included; the more likely it is that some people will be accepted for whom benefits were not intended; the more likely it is that the system will be impersonally operated, in terms of the perception of the clientele, as well as intrinsically; the more inflexibly will the system be operated and the more unresponsive the system will be to the clientele; the less concerned the disbursers of resources will be about the scarcity of funds; the more likely it is that errors will occur; and the greater will be the operational cost per unit. Only in large-scale systems will the administration be required to adhere to a mindless equality among clients when differential treatment may actually be appropriate.

AVOIDING BUREAUCRACY

It may well be that industrial methods of operation are efficient in the production and distribution of mechanical objects, but the experience of the welfare states suggests that this is not the case where welfare or other human behavioural factors are involved. Probably a highly centralised social insurance system is also efficacious if adjudication and distribution can be related to objective unalterable processes. In the matter, however, of issues relating to human behaviour and socio-cultural values, it is only in the small unit of local government that such human questions can be resolved in a consistently humane manner.

DANGERS OF OPPRESSION

The centralised welfare state also presents 'dystopian' dangers, which most people have not considered. As the mechanisms of the welfare-cum-rights-without-responsibility state proceed to promote permissive behaviour without adequate childhood socialisation, increasing concern for high levels of crime and other social pathologies may raise a clamour for improved social control. This, in turn, can lead the way towards highly centralised government and the danger of dictatorship.

We are beginning to see elements of this in the obtrusive investigations of child abuse, child neglect and child incest, under which children have been removed from their homes without court action or recourse, with parental control of children nullified. Cornish for example (1986) discusses licences for parenting! He justifies this proposal by citing studies which have proved that children from homes with strong and supportive parents learn even in a 'bad' school with poor teachers. He notes the great damage done to many children by ineffective parents. He, therefore, presses for parent training and licensing. If a license is needed for driving a car, why not limit the unrestricted freedom to have a child to 'appropriate' parents? He argues that there is already growing central government authority to trace missing fathers and hold them for support and to hold parents responsible for their children's babies. There is already government authority to hold parents responsible for their children's behaviour. It is only rarely enforced, but under Cornish's proposal, this would be more stringently applied. By the use of computerised control it could operate across the whole country. One can reasonably expect then that unless the informal social control of the functional local community can be re-established 'big brother' government is likely to become even more powerful and dangerous.

GEMEINSCHAFT AND GESELLSCHAFT

In order to understand why the Swiss system works, it is essential to examine the differences between the 'objective industrial community' and the 'empathic local community'.

Ferdinand Tönnies (1963) was the first to make the distinction between the commercial community and the organic community. The *Gemeinschaft* community is one in which relationships are intimate, traditional, and informal – a 'folk' society. The *Gesellschaft* society refers to relationships which are contractual, impersonal, voluntary and limited. *Gemeinschaft* relationships represent the 'glue' in our society which hold us together. *Gesellschaft* relationships represent the business processes governed primarily by the economic market.

For a parent to rear a child, *Gemeinschaft* relationships are required. In order to build a factory, *Gesellschaft* relationships are required. If one allows *Gemeinschaft* relationships to shape one's decisions in an industrial programme, one can look forward to bankruptcy. If one seeks to deal with one's close friends strictly on the basis of *Gesellschaft* relationships, one would soon be friendless.

Helping a person to become self-sufficient from a state of dependency requires a kind of relationship which involves a combination of the caring of the *Gemeinschaft* and the businesslike rules of the *Gesellschaft*. Using the rules alone will not work, nor can 'caring' alone be effective. The problem with the welfare state is that it has sought to use only *Gesellschaft* methods, with a purported claim of 'caring' for the clientele in an impersonal, socially distant, rule-ridden relationship.

It is hardly likely that a huge national, centrally organised or centrally controlled welfare system can provide the individualised mix of *Gemeinschaft* and *Gesellschaft* relationship needed by the welfarised clientele or by the unsocialised or deviantly socialised children of the welfarised family. It is equally unlikely that a centralised, nationalised programme, can relate itself to helping with the creation of families, to helping to preserve families, or to helping families accept the disciplines and constraints necessary for their own rehabilitation and for the rearing of their children.

3 The Autonomous Local Community

Only in the autonomous local community can individual rehabilitation goals be addressed; can necessary exceptions be made with specific clients without creating national precedents; can welfare services be arranged providing for local conditions without, at the same time, affecting the rules by which other clients are served in other locations; can a welfare programme be carried out according to the cultural and value patterns of the community – the same cultural and value patterns which the client will have to adhere to after he has attained self-sufficiency. Only in the autonomous local community can a welfare programme be designed which can provide for a prompt appeal mechanism without bureaucratic impediments to resolution of disagreements; can voluntary welfare programmes be integrated with public welfare programmes for rehabilitation; can the total information and resources of the client and community be quickly known and used effectively for rehabilitation; can help be rendered to a citizen by his concerned peers, rather than by some impersonal agency.

In the autonomous local community, it is hardly likely that a person would get lost in the system – as long as the local unit is small enough for *Gemeinschaft* to prevail. Only in the autonomous local community can social work professionals be made responsible for their decisions and accountable to local officials and neighbours. In such a setting, professionals are more likely to be concerned with speedy rehabilitation and client self-sufficiency. Only in a local autonomous community, which carries full responsibility for its citizenry and which has to raise its own money by local taxes, will funds be spent in a manner which is accountable to local taxpayers.

In centralised welfare programmes the community dollar is worth less than 80 cents after it has made the trip to the capital and back. In the autonomous local community this dollar would be worth the entire 100 cents, and even more when one considers the contributions of local volunteers.

Only in the autonomous local community can the norm of reciprocity be enforced under which citizens are expected to serve others as they themselves expect to be served. Only in the autonomous local

107

community can each citizen be called on to do his share of the community's work, and each citizen in turn can receive the benefits of a welfare programme which does not contribute to social unrest. The *Gesellschaft* has *never* been able to deal adequately with issues of personal relationship. Only if we retain the *Gemeinschaft* in our home communities can we retain an atmosphere of economic freedom along with communal and personal responsibility and control.

The complexity of life brought on by the industrial revolution and the new technological revolution make it difficult for us to be concurrently businesslike and humane. It seems increasingly likely that the only alternative to either an inhumane world where we are all subject to an impersonal 'big brother' government managed by universal fear, or an anarchic jungle in which no one is safe, is the development of a society of small, autonomous, and self-reliant communities. Until such an association of autonomous communities and regions can be achieved, we might at least grasp some of the cues offered to us by the Swiss.

4   What the Swiss Have Taught Us

The Swiss have taught us the importance of altruism as a locally effective motivation for good citizenship. We have always known that altruism is related to love, but not too clearly. We know that love for others begins with self-love, in the baby for himself, and, in time, for his parents, his siblings, his playmates, his classmates, and others known to him (or her). Empathy for others is seldom found unless there is human interaction. It expands from self to family, to neighbours, to fellow citizens in one's small community, and, finally, to one's region, to the people in one's nation, and then to other unmet humans.

The force of this concept is brought upon us when disaster strikes a community or region. Only then do many people come forward with help. Often, many of these people have held themselves apart from mutual aid, but when there is a demonstration of a 'common fate' they come forward and provide generous offerings. By tying each citizen to a home community and by keeping these communities small, the average Swiss has achieved a close, direct tie to others. Only when the nation is at war or threatened by external problems are all citizens involved and roused to concern. But, at the local level, such immediate altruism, the attitudes of Swiss citizens to their fellows in need, is similar to one's feelings towards one's siblings – a desire to be realistically helpful and generous, without irresponsibly promoting dependency through licence.

The Swiss have also helped to demonstrate that social problems begin when authority and responsibility are relinquished to central authorities. The Swiss have rejected the theory prevalent in other western nations that the welfare client is always the victim of the system; that in the matter of crime, the culprit is merely a victim of the system; that the user is a helpless victim of the drug supply system; that in workers' compensation cases the employees are always the victims and never responsible themselves for industrial accidents; that in divorce and family break-up, there is anything such as mutual-'no-fault'; or that in relation to social behaviour the deviant is never at fault.

The Swiss seek to examine each individual case, and endeavour not only to help the helpless, but to prevent recurrence by identifying the causes of the problem.

Another lesson of the Swiss experience is that widespread interventionism in social and human services by central government is not necessary in order to resolve and prevent social problems. Instead the proposal of the Bergers (1984, p. 210) for restoration of family autonomy and responsibility as much as possible, as soon as possible, is already firm policy in Switzerland.

A further lesson to be learned from Switzerland is that problems can be resolved only by directly facing them where they occur. The different outcomes in Switzerland compared with the welfare states demonstrate that problems cannot be solved by simply re-defining them. Re-definition of problems, as an alternative to facing up to them, has occurred for example in relation to unmarried motherhood, which has been re-defined as the father-free family. Alcoholism has been re-defined entirely as a disease, rather than as a problem caused by individual behaviour. Aberrant sex has been re-defined as acceptable and even normal behaviour. The need for welfare has been re-defined as mere lack of money, rather than as a condition which needs positive attention. At times indeed even crime has been re-defined as a psychiatric condition, rather than the consequence of individual choice and inadequate socialisation which it is.

The Swiss, by contrast, have shown that these and other problems *can* be controlled effectively – but only by facing them, and holding the basic institutions responsible for teaching socially appropriate and acceptable behaviour. *Constant re-definition of social problems is nothing more than avoidance behaviour, and can do nothing to solve them.*

Moreover, the Swiss experience has demonstrated that it is only at the local level that citizens and decision makers alike can view problems from what DuWors (1952) describes as 'the principle of first definitions'. Only at the local level is it possible for people to arrive at congruent and common definitions of recurring life situations. Poverty, crime, drug addiction, familial dissolution, and other crucial problems can be examined for cause only at the level where common definitions are achievable, and only then is it possible to arrive at effective solutions.

Another important lesson that can be learned from the Swiss is that no one social problem — welfare, unemployment, school dropout, crime, drugs and so on, can be resolved separately. Each of these problems must be attacked in combination at the local level, so that provisions can be individualised and local citizenry involved. Other nations which seek to resolve these problems as effectively as the Swiss can start by returning to local communities their right to tax their citizens and to authorise communities and regions to attack all these problems without national interference.

In the case of problem communities with insufficient resources, some modest mechanism can easily be devised for regional and inter-community support.

The first priority for community work should be prevention of further dependency by training parents and teachers to work toward maximum academic and/or work-ready education. In the emergency period, with thousands of unemployable youth, a plan would need to be devised in each community to prepare youth for employability, with finances for a time provided by the national government. Unearned welfare grants and dole payments, and even unearned social insurances, should be phased out over a period of time, with the goal of eventually returning welfare responsibilities, and authority to local communities.

All in all, what can we learn from the Swiss? Fundamentally this: that human programmes do not function without incentives, and that incentives differ with people and places. The best place (perhaps the only place) where human programmes can be fully effective is in the local community, where people care about each other, where they depend upon each other to keep the peace and to promote each other's well-being, and where children can be brought up to consider their neighbours and to be considered by them.

What the welfare states should learn from their own experiences is that national and central government cannot solve social problems. It is no more able to solve the problems of individuals than are parents able to solve the problems of grown children who live away from home. Parents of grown children know only too well that, even when it is asked for, their help often ends disastrously. Similarly, national government, no matter how well-intentioned, cannot provide the socialisation that only a father and mother can deliver.

Central government everywhere should learn at least that part of the Hippocratic Oath which says '*Above all, do no harm*'. The welfare state and its policies are doing grave harm by making the fathers of many families obsolete and by distorting or destroying the socialisation of children. We should put a stop to this immediately. In *Rebuilding America*, Alperovitz and Faux show conclusively that a large and disparate nation cannot plan centrally without doing serious harm regionally and locally. This is a lesson the welfare state nations should take to heart, as they look perhaps to Switzerland for an alternative approach.

Part IV
Towards Reform of British and American Social Policy

Part IV

1 Welfare State Societies in Decay

Britain and the United States share many fundamental characteristics which serve in combination to distinguish them even from other free societies:

Both countries are stable democracies. Established political institutions are positively supported by the mass of their populations. Anti-democratic forces have little scope for success, and – even in times of severe economic recession – find negligible popular support.

In both countries the independent institutions of the law occupy a central position within the social structure and the established social value system. They operate effectively and equitably, for the most part, in the maintenance of social freedom and public order.

In both countries the institution of private property is securely established, and access to income and wealth is broadly distributed.

In both countries the other key institutions of capitalism are equally well established and broadly supported. These include in particular the competitive pursuit of profit, a free labour market, and restraints on interference with free enterprise either by state organisations or by powerful corporate agencies.

In both countries the population as a whole is intelligent and educated.

In both countries systems of communication and information transmission are powerful and remarkably open. Freedom of opinion, freedom of speech, freedom of association, and the freedom of the press are powerfully institutionalised and intensively utilised. The scope for new and heterogeneous ideas and for consequent social and technical innovation is large.

In both countries GNP, living standards, and quality of life are by historical and contemporary standards alike very high.

However, even with these and other important social characteristics in common, these two great free societies are also enormously different the one from the other. Britain, for example, remains much more ethnically homogeneous than the United States. America is rather less centralised than Britain, with less power available to

115

the central state apparatus. Interference in the economy, through nationalisation or regulation, is trivial in the United States by comparison with Britain. The power and influence of trade unions is much greater in Britain than in the United States. The American population at all levels is much more enterprise-oriented than are British people, and so on.

Not the least of the differences between the two countries is in the extent and nature of state welfare provision. Apart from Bismarck's Prussia, Britain has been the historical pioneer in state welfarism. From the late 19th century onwards, and with explosive escalations in the early 1900s, the 1940s, and during the 1960s and 1970s, British social policy has followed a consistent movement towards increasingly comprehensive, homogeneous and centralised welfare provision. Only in communist societies are there to be found anywhere in the modern world state bureaucracies of the scale created by the British welfare state.

In America, by contrast, despite the New Deal and the Great Society, commitment to State Welfare provision has always been tempered by scepticism about its side-effects and its implications. The strength of faith in market mechanisms and self-help has remained almost as firm in America as it has been weak in Britain since the mid-19th century.

From a certain perspective, the welfare systems of these two societies can only seem dramatically different – the USA representing the archetype of 'residualism' with public welfare provision kept to an absolute minimum, and Britain providing a more complete exemplar of the welfare state in all its Byzantine glory than even Scandinavia.

However, this polarised comparison conceals at least as much as it discloses, and in the last resort it provides a completely inadequate and inaccurate account of the state of welfare in the two societies. For, although the United States may have come much later and for the most part reluctantly to state welfare, in the past 30 years it has moved very rapidly on most social policy fronts in the same dangerous directions as other welfare state societies. In health, housing, social security, poverty management and the rest, US social policy and administrative machinery are now in all essential respects identical with those of older established welfare state societies. In each case, small beginnings restricted to the poorest and weakest sectors of society have expanded to encompass in their bureaucratic tentacles ever broader segments of the population (Hasenfeld and Zald, 1985).

In consequence, what we find in the late 1980s in both these societies is a condition of welfare sclerosis. In both of them bureaucratic state welfare is progressively choking off individual enterprise. Bureaucratic centralism is increasingly preventing the autonomous growth of local initiatives and sapping personal responsibility. Welfarist policies are continually generating more and more dependency, and in consequence escalating the level of apparent need for yet more welfare (Murray, 1984; Seldon, 1981).

As the corporatist and pseudo-socialist ramifications of state welfarism extend their hold, the free institutions of democratic society are progressively undermined, and the chances of maintaining freedom and democracy are inexorably diminished. With ever larger proportions of national wealth and income devoted to state welfare expenditure, real standards of living begin to dwindle, and even in the midst of potential prosperity the objective conditions of beggary are being constructed to suit the beggar-state mentality which state welfarism inevitably creates (Segalman, 1986).

It is in the context of this frightening scenario of free societies driven by irresponsible state welfarism towards economic, social and moral bankruptcy that the electoral triumphs of Mr Reagan and Mrs Thatcher in the 1980s should be seen. Both were elected and re-elected to challenge and reverse the long-term trend we have been describing. Both of them have had some success in relation to this goal. But few even among their most loyal supporters would claim that either of them has so far had anything better than a marginal effect.

Bureaucracy still flourishes. Central state organisations remain dominant in welfare. Public expenditure continues at very high levels. New pauper dependents are being created daily even under their allegedly libertarian auspices in thousands. In Britain and America, as throughout almost the whole of the free world, state welfare is continuing its destructive progress. Some more powerful, more subtle, and more systematic approach than has so far been tried is needed urgently, or soon it will be too late. In the following pages we offer the outlines of such an approach, based on the investigations reported earlier in this book.

2 Reform of Taxation, Incentives and the Work Environment

Our analysis suggests that the major damage caused by state welfare provision is the creation of welfare dependency. As a consequence of the principles, scale, mode of organisation and practical procedures of state welfare provision, large numbers of people who are fully capable of supporting themselves and their dependents effectively cease to do so, and progressively become incapacitated for future independent participation in social life in a free society. This individual dependency is almost inevitably generalised to whole families, and transmitted by inadequate and inappropriate socialisation from one generation to the next.

The antithesis of welfare dependency is social autonomy – the capacity to support oneself, and one's dependents through one's own efforts in the labour market. Fundamental changes in the ways in which work and work incentives are currently handled are essential elements in the reforms which are required to reduce welfare dependency.

It would be foolish of us to suggest that the requisite reforms can be easily or uncontroversially specified, or that, even if a programme of reform were agreed, it could be implemented without difficulty. For example, even among experts convinced, as we are, of the urgent necessity of reforms in the socio-psychological environment of work, there is disagreement about the effects of minimum wage regulations, about the advisability of central state involvement in social insurance, and other important issues (Parker, 1984; Wiseman and Marsland, 1987).

Again there are few, even among those most sceptical about current welfare arrangements, who are unaware that belligerent political resistance to reform is inevitable, given the many vested interests and ideological prejudices involved. For example, a recent examination of attempts since 1979 at welfare reform in Britain interprets them with a cavalier bias as 'the politics of greed' (Loney, 1986). The author can rely on a sympathetic reading of his implausible arguments by many thousands of committed socialists and officeholders within the welfare system. We shall be surprised if resistance to welfare reform in Britain and the USA is significantly easier to overcome than the reactionary bureaucratism faced by Mr Gorbachev in the USSR!

Nonetheless, it seems to us feasible and potentially useful to spell out here our own suggestions about the key reforms we believe are necessary in this sphere. We plan to take up the arguments about their desirability and feasibility in a later publication (Gilder, 1986; Murray, 1984; Parker, 1982 and 1984):–

  amendment of tax thresholds to eliminate 'poverty traps';

  introduction in the longer term of a negative income tax system;

  progressive reduction of all income tax;

  elimination of all income support in kind;

  complete separation of social insurance (for health, pensions, and unemployment) from social assistance to those in unpredictable need;

  encouragement of private and co-operative social insurance for health, unemployment and pensions. Eventually federal or central state involvement should be limited to legal requirement of insurance by all persons and to supervision of private and co-operative schemes;

  reduction of all welfare benefits in relation to available wage levels. It should be in no one's financial interest to remain on benefit unnecessarily;

  elimination of minimum wage regulations (Marsland, 1984);

  gradual replacement of benefit grants by loans. This will both reduce dysfunctional stigma and encourage a quicker return to self-reliance;

  coupling of all welfare benefits, whether grants or loans, to the requirement of involvement in appropriate rehabilitation programmes. The aim should be to restore to welfare recipients their capacity for independent participation in social life. This may involve, for example, further education, job training, health care, or counselling (Segalman, 1986);

  obligatory workfare (useful work in return for benefits) and retraining for the unemployed. Abandonment of unemployed men and women to purposeless inactivity on the dole is as cruel to them as it is destructive of society;

  obligatory requirement for families to support young unemployed people (see the next section for more concerning the family);

improvements in education to encourage enterprising, self-reliant attitudes in young men and women. Currently teachers often have the opposite effect (Brophy, 1985);

financial and administrative responsibility for support and rehabilitation for those in need of help to be delegated to the local community level. Only local responsibility can ensure personal attention, prevent abuses and inhibit the irresponsible 'rights' mentality which depersonalised, large-scale systems invariably produce (on the role of the local community in reducing welfare dependency, see page 125 below);

retraining of social workers and other welfare personnel to adopt attitudes to those in genuine need of help which are supportive of enterprise, self-help, and self-reliance. Currently social workers' anxieties about stigma, their ideological commitment to state welfarism, and their ignorance about the world of work have the effect of actively discouraging their 'clients' from trusting their own capacities and resources and from finding ways of retrieving their autonomy. Welfare personnel are a major cause of welfare dependency (Wiseman & Marsland, 1987, Appendix on social workers).

Without reforms along these lines, the welfare systems of Britain and the USA will continue the inexorable drift which is bringing an increasing proportion of their populations into the state welfare net. Already this has gone a long way towards creating an under-class of merely pseudo-citizens who constitute a dangerous reservoir of apathetic and potentially disaffected serfs. Only the restoration to them of the opportunities for autonomous self-reliance – which all citizens are owed in any genuine democracy – can rescue them from self-destructive subservience, and save our two societies from paralysis and decay. Above all this requires changes such as we have proposed here to provide effective incentives for all citizens to work hard and to encourage in their children enterprising, self-reliant attitudes and a commitment to work as a primary source of identity and worth.

3 Support for the Family

Our reports in earlier pages of this book demonstrate graphically that, if the main direct destructive effect of state welfare is through its impact on work and work attitudes, the primary arena in which its long-term damage is done is the family. If welfare dependency is to be reduced, reforms of the work environment must be accompanied by measures designed to strengthen and support the family as a social institution.

For the family is the crucial – indeed indispensable – mechanism in producing autonomous, self-reliant personalities, capable of resisting the blandishments of welfare dependency. It is apparently only in the context of loving support and rational discipline which the family offers – provided it is intact and functioning effectively – that children can be reliably socialised into the values and skills which social autonomy requires (Gilder, 1981).

Thus anything – be it the welfare dependency of parents, social policies which set a premium on family disruption, or permissive cultural attitudes and irresponsible social role models – anything at all which weakens the fabric of families inevitably generates and escalates welfare dependency. In particular, social policies which make the role of the father redundant, or weaken the legitimate authority of parents in the socialisation of their children, are likely to create environments in which only exceptional children are capable of growing up into genuinely mature, autonomous adults. The vast majority of children reared in broken or inadequate families are headed for welfare dependency in one form or another, and also for other social problems.

Already post-war developments in social welfare policy and trends over the same period (and more especially since the 1960s) in cultural values and life-styles have gone a long way towards destroying the family as a social institution (Anderson & Dawson, 1986). Fundamental changes are required if this process is to be reversed and if the escalation of welfare dependency attributable to the weakness of the family is to be prevented in the future.

Even in communist Russia, it seems, the essential role of the family in the socialisation of children to constructive values and to the social skills required for effective independent participation in social life is being recognised. A recent report (*The Times* (London), August 13,

1987) on homeless children in the USSR concludes as follows:

> Time was in the Soviet Union when the family was considered a subversive unit, because families offered a loyalty that could compete, and might conflict, with loyalty to the state and the Communist Party. Now it is being recognised officially that family life is the foundation of a stable society and state requirements that might conflict with family obligations are being re-examined.

It would be strange indeed if a renewal of awareness about the crucial value of the family were achieved under communism – which is in principle an enemy of the family, rather than in Britain, the USA, and the other democracies – where the family's indispensable significance as a buffer between individual and state, and as the primary source of secure identity and personal autonomy has, until recently, always been emphasised. Sadly, we have been too much and too easily deceived by the family's many ideological enemies, and far too naive about the destructive effects on the family institution of many of our social welfare policies.

Much needs to be done. The following is a short-list of what seems to us crucial. It will be obvious to the reader that our proposals concerning the family are more contentious and more difficult to achieve even than the measures suggested earlier in relation to welfare and work. For the most part they are better classified as cultural changes than as policy reforms, and in the nature of things, the latter are much more amenable – even in the face of resistance – to rational implementation than the former.

Our programme for cultural change with respect to the family is therefore perhaps better read as an agenda for debate than as a programme of reform. This, however, renders it not one iota less important. We are convinced, on the basis of the investigations reported in this book, and our broader studies of the destructive effects of recent changes in family relations, that the problem of welfare dependency cannot be addressed adequately unless the level and nature of support provided for the family by the state is transformed dramatically. For four decades and more, public energies and resources in Britain and America have been devoted to the destruction of the family. This must be halted and reversed if democracy is to be preserved, to which end the following are essential:

> implementation of the reforms of work and welfare described earlier (pages 118–20). The family cannot survive and thrive unless

its natural and necessary economic responsibilities and moral authority are restored to it by these reforms;

careful reconsideration of policy in relation to one-parent families. Avoiding unnecessary stigma is one thing; providing positive incentives for the proliferation of incomplete and inadequate families is another;

amendments in legislation designed to reduce the rate of divorce. Despite re-marriage, divorce is a major source of inadequate socialisation of children, and therefore of welfare dependency;

improvements in marriage and family education, and in support services to help married couples with difficulties;

critical analysis of school and college text books and teaching which are prejudiced and subversive in relation to the family as an institution;

serious attention to damaging role models in the media and public life in relation to promiscuity, adultery and homosexuality. The re-moralisation of social life need neither be a merely reflex response to AIDS, nor an authoritarian and reactionary expression of fundamentalist 'Ayatollism'. Re-moralisation in a modern and democratic form is absolutely vital if the family's health is to be restored;

as a further and broader aspect of this same endeavour, analysis of the values, attitudes, and life-styles associated with the so-called 'permissive society';

research and policy development in relation to youth peer groups and their role in influencing young people's sexual behaviour, moral attitude and work values (Marsland, 1982);

innovative thinking about the scope for retrieving three-generation family units (for example, in relation to house-building patterns and tax incentives for family care of the elderly);

research to identify measures which, without blocking the career aspirations of women, would limit the damaging effects on children of dual careers, overtime working, and 'workaholism', e.g. tax rebates for child-caring wives;

tax incentives and other encouragements for family enterprises. As Gilder's analysis suggests, joint family involvement in business is a major stimulus to entrepreneurial action, and by the same token a powerful antidote against falling into welfare dependency. (Gilder, 1981 and 1986). The case of Greek Cypriot immigrants to Britain demonstrates the effectiveness of family businesses in

providing even disadvantaged people rapidly with the capacities
and resources needed for self-reliance (Oakley 1982).

We believe the agenda constituted by these proposals may offer a
useful framework for the thorough-going debate about the family
which is needed. For far too long the family has been subverted and
dismissed on grossly prejudiced and scientifically inadequate grounds
by influential Marxist, socialist and feminist critics. Far from being,
as its enemies argue, a repressive 'bourgeois' institution – responsible
for patriarchal oppression of women, unjust subjugation of children,
and inhibition of social change and 'liberation' – *the family is the
indispensable seedbed of genuine freedom.* It is from the care and
discipline which the family reliably provides, if it is not sabotaged by
wrong-headed social policies, that mature, autonomous people grow,
men and women with the capacities for living as free people, immune
to welfare dependency.

4 Reinvigorating the Local Community

Our analysis of the Swiss case – the only major exception in the free world to the general descent into welfare dependency – suggests a third major dimension in the framework of social characteristics necessary to the maintenance of social freedom and personal autonomy. To sensible welfare policies which encourage economic self-reliance by protecting work incentives, and to powerful cultural support for the autonomy and authority of the family, must be added delegation of real independence and power to local communities.

Localism is an indispensable bastion against state welfarism and welfare dependency, while centralism provides the normal, and perhaps necessary, context for the elaborated and oppressive bureaucracy on which state welfarism feeds. Only in a context of close interpersonal interaction and extensive mutual acquaintance is it possible to maintain that sense of common identity and shared responsibility which prevents people from becoming mere passengers in social life, parasitical and subservient 'free riders' on the efforts of others.

Where, on the contrary, the conditions of 'mass society' prevail, with individuals atomised, and mutual bonds of acquaintance and dependence diminished, where social relations are wholly bureaucratised and depersonalised, and initiative, power, and responsibility are located in a distant centre – these are the conditions in which state welfarism and welfare dependency flourish, and the freedom and self-reliance of genuine democracy are threatened by the multiple problems which welfare dependency invariably causes.

Now of course there is no way that large-scale, industrialised societies can turn back the clock to retrieve the conditions – in any case largely mythical – of Tönnies' *Gemeinschaft*. This, however, is no reason why societies such as Britain and America should not seek to organise social arrangements so as to minimise the extent of gross centralism and guarantee to local communities major responsibilities. Among the many benefits of thorough-going localism not the least would be effective control of welfare and a substantial reduction in welfare dependency.

In this respect, the USA is already at a great advantage compared with Britain. For the federal constitution reserves considerable real power for the States, and in and of itself this prevents the worst excesses of centralised societies such as Britain and France. It is no accident that Switzerland has a federal structure, as to a lesser extent does West Germany, which is also a prosperous country with a lesser dependency problem than most advanced societies.

We believe it would make a good deal of sense – in relation to welfare policy as much as in other fields – for Britain to move towards a modest degree of federalism by devolving power to Scotland, Wales and five or six English provinces. This is not a novel proposal and indeed it has figured in the manifesto of the Alliance parties for some time. Moreover, political support for devolution is potentially strong at present as a result of widespread feelings of discontent in several of the provincial regions.

Even this degree of devolution is not, however, likely to be sufficient to answer the problems of centralism in relation to welfare arrangements. California has a population of more than 20 million. English regional provinces might have populations as large in some cases as 8 to 10 million. The key issue is at a much lower level of population, and concerns local government proper, and the mode of organisation adopted in the conurbations.

In the rural areas and other areas of low population density, this problem is not too difficult. Here coherently bounded areas with reasonably small populations are readily enough identified. It is in the heavily urbanised, densely populated zones of the big cities and the massive conurbations that argument and political dissension about the optimum boundaries for local government seem almost beyond rational resolution (Hall, 1979).

One thing at least seems certain in the 1980s. The days when big was assumed to be best, and the alleged economies and efficiencies of scale were taken glibly for granted, have gone for good. In relation to welfare as much as in relation to education, health, housing and perhaps even planning and transportation, maximum devolution of power to real communities of not more than a quarter of a million is what we would prefer to see.

These local community units – the equivalent of Switzerland's cantons – ought to be financially self-supporting to the maximum possible extent. The routine payment by central government in Britain of 60 and 70 per cent of the expenditures of local authorities has done more than anything else to destroy genuine localism. Only financial autonomy and responsibility can guarantee local initiative and enterprise, responsible local policies and the sort of local community authority which the excision of welfare dependency requires.

If responsibility for welfare – with the vast bulk of current provision transferred first to private and co-operative institutions – were reposed entirely in the authority of these small local communities, the whole texture of its administration would be radically changed for the better. Instead of the current exclusive emphasis on 'rights', the balance would shift towards responsibilities. Where currently many benefits are doled out unthinkingly on an impersonal basis, there would be a move towards working out personalised programmes for particular individuals and families. Where at present problem individuals and families are typically ignored until their difficulties have become too serious for much to be done about them, the close, informal supervision of the local community would instead identify problems early, and ensure that useful steps were taken to help. Instead of the current homogeneous blanket system of welfare provision, providing universal benefits regardless of real need and without proper attention to their appropriateness in different situations, we should see much greater variability from one community to another. It would be much healthier if different policies with varying levels and types of provision were established by different communities, allowing comparison, competition and evolutionary change.

However, this last point also suggests an apparent danger which local community autonomy might threaten. Since the 1960s in Britain, it has been particular local authorities – the Greater London Council, extreme left-wing councils in the north of England, such as the so-called 'Socialist Republic of South Yorkshire' – which have installed the most profligate policies, and done most to increase the extent of welfare dependency. It could be argued that with increased freedom and power for local communities, there would be even more such damaging folly.

While the danger is certainly real, we believe the risk is worth taking, and indeed must be taken. If local people are required to pay for their own policies, *with no chance of being baled out by central government*, they will soon recognise mischievous nonsense when they see it, and elect different leaders. Our whole approach presumes – and it is an assumption backed by considerable evidence – that where people have a real and visible stake in their community, they will involve themselves seriously, and take action to ensure that local resources – their own money – are not wasted, and that the lives and energies of their neighbours and fellow citizens are not squandered by destructive welfare arrangements. This strategy requires that local communities should be restored to genuine autonomy. Without the risk of error this involves, there is no chance at all of transforming them into the nurseries of personal initiative and individual self-reliance they need to become.

5   Reform in Housing and Education

There are two further areas of social policy where radical reform is necessary if the British and American people are to leave welfare dependency well and truly behind them. These are *housing* and *education* – two fields in which the seeds of welfare dependency currently grow and flourish profusely.

Ironically, both housing and education have long been favourite targets for well-meaning philanthropists and over-confident social engineers. The history books and reform bills are full of graphic descriptions of the squalid housing conditions of the poor, and their ignorance has been blamed for much of the suffering they have had to endure. New housing and good schools have been the recommended panacea of the interfering classes for generations. Yet what do we find in the inner cities of our two countries as the century draws to its close? Sprawling, high-rise tenement projects with doors and windows boarded up, on streets which even policemen visit nervously at best; where addicts, muggers and burglars roam freely, and nullify for thousands the security which home and only home can provide; where litter, graffiti and vandalism on every hand display the careless unconcern of residents for their own neighbourhoods (Coleman, 1985).

And in the schools? Truancy exists on a huge and grossly underestimated scale. There is sullen disaffection against every educational ideal. Bored and bullied or bullying pupils are common. Domination by the nihilistic culture of pop and rampant permissivism is prevalent. Broken teachers are becoming the norm. The educational dream has become a hopeless nightmare (Anderson, Marsland, and Lait, 1981).

In these two areas of the neighbourhood and the school, new welfare dependents are being created month by month and year by year. Individuals and families are having the spirit of enterprise and the will to organise their own lives knocked out of them. Hundreds of thousands of our fellow citizens are being shaped for nothing but subservient pauperism, and all in the name of planning and progress. Even the radical changes in work and welfare, the family and the local community we have recommended earlier will fail unless they are accompanied by a new approach to housing and to education.

129

In New York, Detroit and Los Angeles, as in London, Liverpool and Glasgow, public housing built as recently as the 1960s and 1970s is being demolished: from slum to slum in 15 years. If these breeding grounds of crime and welfare dependency are to be eliminated once and for all a whole new strategy for housing is needed:

outlaw absolutely any building or administration of housing by public authorities;

eliminate all funding of housing by public authorities except in the form of tax rebates or loans to individuals, co-operatives, or private companies;

eliminate all housing benefit grants and housing aid which leaves residents unaware of the real costs of their homes;

encourage, by the provision of protected loans, the establishment of small-scale co-operative home building, home purchase, and home renting schemes, and self-help housing;

encourage, through tax rebates, the establishment of home purchase loan schemes for employees and members of companies, trade unions and so on;

phase out rent controls – a primary cause of homelessness (Tucker, 1987);

local communities to provide loans for home maintenance and improvement;

increase expenditure on local policing and community self-defence;

increase expenditure on local youth service and youth involvement programmes, and youth employment training schemes.

If housing policy were transformed along these radical lines, the whole quality of neighbourhood life in our inner cities would be rapidly improved. It would offer to poorer citizens a real stake in their local communities, and an opportunity for them and their families to gain for the first time the benefits of a genuine home in which they could rationally invest care and pride.

The main role of the family in preventing welfare dependency is to provide a context of care, support and discipline within which children can learn the attitudes and skills required for self-reliant living. The role of the schools is to build on this foundation and carry it further. In Britain and America they are patently failing in this role abysmally, especially with children of average and less than average ability. The evidence of this failure is extensive and indisputable (Brophy, 1985; O'Keeffe, 1986).

Here let it suffice to consider a report of two recent studies (*Mail on Sunday*, 16 August 1987). A study of 15-year-olds, given mathematics tests involving decimals, fractions and percentages, found that West German children did twice as well as British children. Indeed many of the British children could not answer the questions at all. In a follow-up study:

Three papers for GCSE Arithmetic were set in a German school for the lowest ability range. A staggering 40 per cent of 15-year-old 'low ability' Hauptschule pupils sailed through the test with marks of 80 to 100 per cent.

That is the equivalent to an O-level grade C pass in this country, achieved by only the top 15 per cent of 16-year-olds. And Hauptschule are the lowest of the three grades of German senior schools, roughly the equivalent of our old secondary modern.

For their six-part programme, Educating Britain, which starts next Sunday, LWT tested British pupils in a similar ability range on the mathematics paper for the Hauptschule leaving certificate. All ten questions on fractions, percentages and decimals have been covered in lessons in the comprehensives.

The 170 British childrens' average mark was 33 per cent compared to the Germans' 61 per cent. Most Germans easily divided 543.75 by 12.5 whereas few of the British pupils knew how to start.

Amazingly a British expert is reported as criticising the German leaving exam as 'too mechanical', and aimed merely at 'cramming mathematical techniques'. Invited to provide an alternative:

. . . she devised her own test, designed to measure pupils' underlying understanding of mathematical principles and how to apply them to practical circumstances.

Again Britain lagged behind. The average German score was 62 per cent compared with 44 per cent in this country.

In Britain and America alike it has fortunately been recognised at last that the fashionable educational platitudes of the past three decades are failing our children. Experiments in tightening up educational objectives and school management; better training of teachers; re-introducing discipline and competition; linking school work with the real world; and involving parents and the local community in the educational process are going ahead rapidly on many fronts.

It is our view that these reforms must be pressed hard in the face of the educational establishment's predictable defensive protestations. Substantial improvements in education are essential if welfare dependency is to be reduced, and if a new generation of young people is to be produced which is better capable of independent, self-disciplined, self-reliant living. Comparisons between American schooling and Japanese, and between British schooling and German, should be continued systematically until the shameful gap is closed. And even then we shall need to make comparisons with Switzerland, where, more even than in Japan or Germany, excellent schooling makes a major contribution to maintaining the mature capacity and personal freedom of Swiss people of all ranks.

6 Towards a Culture of Freedom

The damaging consequences of the welfare policies adopted all over the Western world after the Second World War are now apparent. Governments of left and right alike are reaching around for solutions to the decay and chaos which increasingly characterise all our major cities. Our argument is that nothing less than a reversal of these policies is necessary if we are to avoid a deepening crisis. The welfare state has proved a damaging distraction and shown itself dangerously counter-productive wherever it has been tried. Instead, we should follow the clues provided by the Swiss, by common sense, and by principles long established in free societies, to reach beyond the welfare state towards real welfare.

In this last part of our book we have briefly outlined a strategy which could lead our two countries in this direction – away from dangerous fantasies towards real welfare. It will require bold political leadership at national level, and both courage and trust on the part of the people. It will demand skill and patience from administrators and local community leaders.

However, the alternative to these difficult challenges is an imposition which, for free people, is infinitely worse – a vicious circle of growing welfare dependency, increasing state control, deepening poverty, worsening anarchy in the inner city, and inexorably diminishing freedom.

If this fate is to be avoided, all the reforms we have proposed are urgently necessary:

> fundamental changes in the structure of work and welfare, to increase personal self-reliance (pages 118–20);
> restoration and augmentation of the autonomy and authority of the family (pages 121–24);
> delegation of central state power and responsibilities to the local community (pages 125–28);
> reform of housing and improvement in the quality of local neighbourhoods (pages 129–30);
> radical changes in education to improve its effectiveness (pages 130–32).

In combination, these reforms will inaugurate a qualitative transformation of the culture of British and American society. Their motivational effects will facilitate a radical shift from the culture of serfdom, into which we have gradually sunk since the Second World War as a result of state welfarist policies, political ineptitude and moral blindness, towards the culture of freedom, in which our two countries have long been pioneers (Marsland, 1988).

Even in the heartlands of socialism in the USSR and China, the past decade has seen a reluctant recognition that all-enveloping state provision from cradle to grave is inefficient and morally dangerous. Here in the powerhouse of freedom and democracy, this is a lesson we should not have needed to learn at all, since it is a corollary of freedom and an axiom of democracy.

For while democracy can restore freedom to people who have been robbed of it, freedom and democracy can neither grow spontaneously nor survive successfully except, and unless, men behave as free men must – that is, freely, independently and with brave self-reliance. The apparatus of state welfare, with whatever beneficent intentions it may be established, necessarily and inevitably inhibits the responsible, adaptable behaviour which freedom requires. Its bureaucratic structures strangle the natural, spontaneously developing co-operative institutions on which freedom depends, the family, the market and the local community foremost among them. Its tangled systems of rules and obligations destroy the capacities of free men and women to choose freely for themselves and to pursue rational interests. Its illegitimate seizure of moral control abandons the people to purposeless drifting, subservient dependency, and aimless incapacity to choose and act for themselves morally, responsibly and freely. Its grip on our two countries and our people must be broken once and for all.

Bibliography

Alperovitz, Gar and Jeff Faux (1984) *Rebuilding America: A Blueprint for the New Economy* (New York: Pantheon Books).

Anderson, D. C. and G. Dawson (eds) (1986) *Family Portraits* (Social Affairs Unit).

Anderson, D. C., D. Marsland and J. Lait (1981) *Breaking the Spell of the Welfare State* (Social Affairs Unit).

Auletta, Ken (1982) *The Under Class* (New York: Random House).

Berger, Brigitte and Peter (1984) *The War Over the Family: Capturing the Middle Ground* (Garden City, N.Y.: Anchor-Doubleday).

Besharov, Douglas J. (1986) 'Unfounded allegations: A new child abuse problem', *The Public Interest*, no. 83, Spring, pp. 18–33.

Bethell, Tom (1985) 'British views and prospects', *The American Spectator*, July, pp. 7–9.

Bethell, Tom (1986) 'Das kapital ideas: II', *The American Spectator*, July, pp. 11–13, 48.

Bourdieu, P. (1980) 'Cultural reproduction and social reproduction', in J. Karabel and A. H. Halsey (eds), *Power and Ideology in Education* (New York and London: Oxford University Press).

Brophy, M. *et al.* (1985) *Trespassing: Businessmen's Views on the Education System* (Social Affairs Unit).

Brown, Muriel and Nicola Madge (1982) *Despite the Welfare State: Studies in Deprivation and Disadvantage* (London: Heinemann Educational Books).

Caldwell, Taylor (1965) *A Pillar of Iron* (Greenwich, Connecticut: Fawcett) p. 572.

Carlson, Allan C. (1983) 'What happened to the family wage?', *The Public Interest*, no. 83, Spring, pp. 3–17.

Clinard, Marshall (1978) *Cities without Crime: the Case of Switzerland* (London: Cambridge University Press).

Coleman, A. (1985) *Utopia on Trial* (Hilary Shipman).

Coleman, J. S., *et al.* (1966) *Equality of Educational Opportunity* (Washington, DC: US Office of Education, Dept. of HEW).

Cornish, Edward (1986). 'Will "parent licenses" protect children?', *Los Angeles Times*, 10 Oct., pt. V, p. 14.

Daniels, A. M. (1986) 'National health goes sick', *The Spectator*, 9 Aug., pp. 8–9.

Davis, Stan Gebler (1986). 'The caring state that ruins us', *The Spectator*, 16 Aug., pp. 14–15.

Dornbusch, Sanford M., Michael J. Fraleigh, Philip L. Ritter, *et al.* (1986) *A Report to the National Advisory Board on the Main Findings of our Collaborative Study of Families and the Schools* (Stanford, CA: Sociology Dept., Stanford University, 27 Feb).

DuWors, Richard E. (1952) 'Persistence and change in local values of two New England communities', *Rural Sociology*, vol. 17, no. 3, Sept., pp. 207–17.

Eisenstadt, S. N. (1985) 'Introduction', in S. N. Eisenstadt and Ora Ahimer, *The Welfare State and Its Aftermath* (Totowa, N.J.: Barnes & Noble).

Forman, Rachel Zinober (1982). *Let Us Now Praise Obscure Women: A Comparative Study of Publicly Supported Unmarried Mothers in Government Housing in the US and Britain* (Washington, D.C.: University Press of America).

Fondation pour la Recherche Sociale (1980) *Poverty and the Anti Poverty Policies: The French Report Presented to the Commission of the European Communities* (Paris: Fondation pour la Recherche Sociale, Dec).

Freeman, Roger A. (1981). *A Preview and Summary of the Wayward Welfare State* (Stanford, CA: The Hoover Institution Press) p. 102.

Gallagher, Maggie (1986) 'Gimme shelter: Children on the run', *National Review* 10 Oct., pp. 38–40.

Gilder, George (1981) *Wealth and Poverty* (Buchan and Enright).

Gilder, George (1986) *The Spirit of Enterprise* (Penguin).

Gilder, George (1986) 'The sexual revolution at home', *The National Review* 10 Oct., pp. 30–4.

Glazer, Nathan (1983) 'Towards a self-service society', *The National Interest*, no. 70, Winter, pp. 66–90.

Green, D. G. (1985) *Which Doctor?* (Institute of Economic Affairs).

Gress, David (1982). 'Daily life in the Danish welfare state', *The Public Interest*, no. 69, Fall, pp. 33–44.

Gruner, Erich (1982) Private correspondence with Segalman, 26 March.

Gurny, Ruth *et al.* (1983) *Careers and Blind Alleys: Paths to Professional Life in the City of Zurich* (Soziologisches Institut der Universität Zürich).

Hall, P. (1977) *The Containment of Urban England* (London: Allen & Unwin, 1973).

Hasenfeld, Y. and M. N. Zald (eds) (1985) *The Welfare State in America: Trends and Prospects* (Annals of the American Academy of Political and Social Science).

Hinde, R. A. (1980) 'Family influences', in M. Rutter, (ed.), *Scientific Foundations of Developmental Psychiatry* (London: Heinemann).

Hirschi, Travis (1983), 'Crime and the family', in James Q. Wilson (ed.), *Crime and Public Policy* (San Francisco: Institute for Contemporary Studies) pp. 53–68.

Jencks, C., *et al.* (1973) *Inequality: A Reassessment of the Effect of Family and Schooling in America* (London: Allen Lane).

Levenstein, Aaron (1964) *Why People Work: Changing Incentives in a Troubled World* (New York: Collier).

Loney, M. (1986) *The Politics of Greed* (Pluto Press).

Luscher, Kurt (1982) 'Fifty years of family policy in Switzerland', in *Profamilia* (Report of the Family Conference of 21 Nov. 1981) (Lucerne: Profamilia Eidgenössischen Verband).

Luscher, Kurt K., Verena Ritter and Peter Gross (1973) *Early Child Care in Switzerland* (London: Gordon & Breach).

Marsland, D. (1982) *Youth, Freedom, and Authority* (Problems of Youth, no. 4).

Marsland, D. (1984) 'The Wages Councils and Unemployment', *Economic Affairs*, vol. 4, no. 2.

Marsland, D. (1988) *Seeds of Bankruptcy: Sociological Bias against Business and Freedom* (Claridge Press).

Meyer, Jürg (1974) *Armut in der Schweiz* (Poverty in Switzerland) (Zurich: Theologischer Verlag).

Mitscherlich, Alexander (1970) *Society without the Father* (New York: Schocken Books).

Mount, Ferdinand (1986) 'Hippies, workfare and the myth of total mobilization', *The Spectator*, 14 June, p. 6.

Murray, Charles (1984) *Losing Ground: American Social Policy, 1950–1980* (New York: Basic Books).

Newhouse, John (1986) 'The gamefish', *New Yorker*, 10 Feb. pp. 68–99.

Nisbet, Robert (1986) book review of *The Rise and Fall of New York City*, by Roger Starr (New York: Basic Books, 1986), in *The American Spectator*, July pp. 43–4.

Oakley, R. (1982) 'Cypriot Families', chapter 10 in R. Rapoport (ed.), *Families in Britain* (London: Routledge & Kegan Paul).

O'Keeffe, D. (ed.) (1986) *The Wayward Curriculum* (Social Affairs Unit).

Parker, H. (1982) *The Moral Hazards of Social Benefits* (Institute of Economic Affairs).

Parker, H. (1984) *Action on Welfare* (Social Affairs Unit).

Pavalko, Ronald M. (1971) *Sociology of Occupations and Professions* (Itaska, Ill.: Peacock).

Reist, W. and Regula Wagner (1982) 'On the Drug Problem in Switzerland', *Zeitschrift für Öffentliche Fürsorge*, Feb., pp. 162–6.

Riesman, D. (1950) *The Lonely Crowd* (Yale University Press).

Rydenfelt, Sven (1981) *The Rise and Decline of the Swedish Welfare State* (Lund, Sweden: Nationalekonomiska Institutionen, Lunds Universitat).

Schaber, Gaston (1980) *Pauvreté Persistant / Grande Région (Project #20)* (Walferdange, Grand Duché de Luxembourg: Group Etude pour les Problèmes de la Pauvreté, July 7).

Segalman, Ralph and Asoke Basu (1981) *Poverty in America: The Welfare Dilemma* (Westport: Greenwood).

Segalman, Ralph (1986) *The Swiss Way of Welfare* (Praeger).

Seldon, A. (1981) *Whither the Welfare State* (Institute of Economic Affairs).

Sharff, Jagna Wojcicka (1981) 'Free enterprise and the ghetto family', *Psychology Today*, vol. 15, no. 4, March.

Sheehan, Susan (1976) *A Welfare Mother* (New York: New American Library, Mentor).

Starr, Roger (1986) *The Rise and Fall of New York City* (New York: Basic Books).

Strang, Heinz (1970) *Erscheinungsformen der Social Hilfebedürftigkeit: Beitrag zur Geschichte, Theorie und Empirischen Analyse der Armut* (Stuttgart: Ferdinande Enke Verlag).

Strang, Heinz (1984) *Sozialhilfebedürftigkeit: Struktur- Ursachen- Wirkung unter besonderer Berücksichtigung der Effektivität der Sozialhilfe* (Forschungsbericht), (Hannover: Institut für Sozialpädagogik der Hochschule-Hildesheim).

Tönnies, Ferdinand (1963) *Community and Society: Gemeinschaft and Gesellschaft* (C. P. Loomis (ed.), New York: Harper).

Trimborn, Harry (1982) 'Switzerland Faces Up to the Growing Problem with Hard Drugs', *Los Angeles Times*, 15 Dec., pt IB, p. 1.

Townsend, Peter (1979) *Poverty in the United Kingdom* (Berkeley: University of California Press).

Tucker, William (1986) 'The landlord's tale', *The New Republic*, 7 July, pp. 14–16.

Tucker, William (1986) 'Moscow on the Hudson', *The American Spectator*, July, pp. 19—21.

Tucker, William (1987) 'Where do the Homeless come from?', *National Review*, 25 Sept.

Van der Vat, Dan (1980) 'Sunderland: Where unemployment is a way of life', *The Times*, 9 June, p. 11.

Van Doorn, Jacques (1978) 'Welfare state and welfare society: the Dutch experience', *Netherlands Journal of Sociology*, 14, pp. 1–8.

Waugh, Auberon (1985) 'Runcieballs revisited, or what to do with the Beveridge Boys', *The Spectator*, 21/28 Dec., p. 9.

Wilensky, Harold L. (1975) *The Welfare State and Equality: Structured and Ideological Roots of Public Expenditures* (Berkeley: University of California Press).

Wilson, William Julius (1985) 'The crisis of the ghetto underclass and the liberal retreat', annual *Social Service Review* lecture, University of Chicago, May.

Wiseman, J. and D. Marsland (1987) *The Social Welfare Programme of the Republic of China* (Taipei: Council for Economic Planning and Development).

Zellman, Gail and Steven L. Schlossman (1986) 'The Berkeley youth wars', *The Public Interest*, no. 84, Summer, pp. 29–41.

Index